The Office Zoo

The Office Zoo

*A guide to survival at the bottom of the hierarchy
in today's high-tech workplace.*

by Lee Wellington

The Office Zoo

A guide to survival at the bottom of the hierarchy in today's high-tech workplace.

2nd Edition
print ISBN: 978-0-9911227-0-7
ebook ISBN: 978-0-9911227-1-4

Text set in Bembo.
Book design and prepress by Kate Weisel, Bellingham, WA
weiselcreative.com

Cover art: *King of the Bachelor Herd*, ©Mary Paquet

The Office Zoo is available as an ebook on Kindle;
in print at Amazon.com; and at my Createspace eStore
https://www.createspace.com/4516724
(where I make the most royalties).

This book is dedicated to my mother

Mom — I love you

1957

Contents

Introduction

The journey which lay before me had staggering logistical requirements. Rommel, Patton, Sun Tzu — their skills were trivial compared to what was needed right now. The "Desert Fox" never had to maneuver in such tight quarters. Patton never had to deal with the consequences of tactlessness toward people who sat mere inches away, day after day, watching every move, breathing the same air, their constant observation affording no possible way to plot and plan while unobserved. Sun Tzu? Forget it. Maybe "After crossing a river, you should get far away from it" was good advice if it was possible — but if you live on the river bank and will need to cross back and forth over the river repeatedly, lots of luck with that one.

It was the middle of the afternoon. My next meeting was in twenty minutes. It would take about ten minutes to prepare my part of the discussion for presentation. However, due to the soft drink at lunch and a few stops at the water fountain I now had to get to the bathroom on the other side of the cube farm — that cavernous open area housing hundreds of worker bees — and back within ten minutes in order to have time to get ready. Pit stops were a lot easier when the meeting was in a conference room — you could just stop at a restroom on the way.

The time I'd spent on this floor gave me great insight into the potential traps and resulting delays that my trip might entail. As was true in many workplaces, most days my coworkers and I spent more time with each other than with our families. Sitting practically in each others' laps, overhearing conversations, seeing who ate what and when, unavoidably witnessing how the myriad situations work entails were handled, gave all of us what was probably more information about each other than we really wanted.

Who really feels comfortable knowing that there are twenty pairs of ears listening to what you say, and how you say it, after a frustrating hour on the phone to a help center in another country, trying vainly to communicate with someone who doesn't speak your language? Though we all had cell phones and could walk outside to make personal calls, we still had to listen to each other during conference calls and conversations that took place in our cubes. Like it or not, we got to know each other pretty well.

Preparing to head for my goal I pondered some details of the minefields and quicksand patches that would have to be evaded or dealt with. Plans for my trip had to be carefully thought out. I stood up and scanned the floor with the eye of a quarterback looking downfield to assess the possibilities, checking the location of key players and making some quick calculations. Who would require a bit of thoughtful maneuvering to avoid? Was there an available route that would only involve going past coworkers unlikely to present problems? Like the quarterback, I needed to process information quickly and make immediate decisions about how to proceed.

At the first cube on the right, an incessant talker lurked. No way to avoid him, since my cube-de-sac deadended to the left. He was alone right now which was unfortunate, since once he snared a victim other people could usually walk by without encountering his standard conversational tripwire of "Hey, I just found out something critical you need to know about..." followed by twenty minutes of a worthless monologue delivered so seamlessly that it was close to impossible to interrupt or escape. I decided to try holding a cell phone to my ear as I walked by and peer distractedly at the other side of the floor. Avoiding eye contact was critical. By doing this, and walking very quickly, getting past his cubicle was generally possible. I made a mental note to bring in earphones to wear on future trips, a strategy I'd seen other potential victims employ successfully.

Next up though, at the left turn leading to the restroom was a quagmire known in the workplace as a "help vampire." The trap was usually set this way: could she just ask me one quick question? This wasn't working; she knew I could fix the problem, as I'd helped her with something similar before. Could I just take one minute to look at it? She was stuck until this was taken care of. If necessary she would have her manager call my manager, who would probably just order me to drop what I was doing and help her anyway, so could I just fix it right now and spare both of us an escalation to management? Knowing that her "one quick question" usually turned into at least thirty minutes of assistance, and that any attempt at an excuse to beg off of helping her would trigger a snit fit I didn't really feel like dealing with right now, I made the decision to turn right instead of left and take the long way to my goal.

And so my trip went. Past the office gossip who mistakenly thought her offer of some "very interesting" information about "someone we both know" would stop me in my tracks, past the manager who had called the meeting, pointedly looking at his watch then back at me, past the self-appointed office "monitor," always closely watching who was away from their desk and for how long. She glanced at me and then at the clock, mentally starting the "away from her cube" timer running.

It couldn't have been much different if I was trying to find a path through a wilderness filled with an assortment of animals which could all be perilous in different ways. Getting past them depended on knowing each animal and coming up with an effective way to negotiate safe passage through their territory.

As I carefully made my way to the restroom and back it occurred to me that, like a real zoo, it would be helpful to have signs outside the cubes announcing something about each person — their characteristics, their habits, and how to deal with them.

Wouldn't it be useful to have information like: "Beware: Occupant of this cube has extreme persecution complex. Any and all conversations will be interpreted to mean other employees are favored and given unfair advantage. While dealing with this person be prepared to listen to repetitive complaints of unequal treatment" posted next to the cube? We have laws requiring truth in advertising, truth in lending, and truth in nutritional labeling, so why not something to help us deal with coworkers?

This would be especially helpful for new people, as they are the ones who can so easily and inadvertently wind up giving offense to the hypersensitive, being detained for hours by the endless talkers, fielding hard-to-turn-down requests to join the softball team or chess club, or being importuned to donate to that really worthy cause — a cause so important that those who refuse to give must be insensitive monsters.

The new hires' initial impulse to try to fit in and get along puts them at a disadvantage in saying no — something which can be sensed by predatory current employees. What better time to get unsuspecting new coworkers to say "yes" to something than before they know better? Projects are assigned this way, so why not requests to participate in extracurricular activities?

This book contains a few thoughts on some of the types of creatures who inhabit our workplaces, along with suggestions for dealing with them and a few words of appreciation about their potential good points, which can be easy to overlook.

In extreme situations moving on is the best way to cope, but in others a good understanding and careful planning can be helpful in getting through the day while still keeping a grasp on sanity, if that is a realistic and possible goal. I say "if" since, in one of the ways that work imitates real life, the options available to deal with the quirks and tics of the people around you depend a lot on your relative place in the pecking order.

A request to turn down a radio or cut back on the swearing will be received much differently when made by someone who will be writing your review or deciding who to lay off than the same request from a peer or subordinate. And sometimes even the most reasonable request is out of the question due to either a low position in the power structure or an assessment of the possible reaction. Do you really want to deal with the consequences of asking someone with a hair-trigger temper to start covering his mouth when he coughs at meetings?

Like the "Jungle Cruise" at Disneyland, as well as a tour showing creatures that need some forethought to deal with, I'll also point out the more benign, but interesting types of coworkers and features in the environment. Most workplaces have at least something of a bachelor herd and a set of competent but under-the-radar minions quietly but efficiently pulling on their oars. Instant communications, while not a human feature of the workscape, can have as detrimental an effect on getting work done as even the most irritating live pest.

A long and interesting career working in development and support for Silicon Valley information technology companies has given me not only a front-row seat to some of the most fascinating advancements of the last few decades, but also to the people creating, maintaining and using that technology. The pace of work and frequency of job changes is probably less intense in other places, since The Valley is also informally known as "Type A Central" — we can be pretty hyper. As a woman in a field that even now continues to be overwhelmingly populated by men I've also gotten a good look at, and a good understanding of, why that is.

Although my experience is in one type of company, friends working in other areas assure me that the cast of characters is similar everywhere, meaning we could all benefit from thinking about how to identify and cope with them, and how to determine when, if there are unavoidable negative effects on mental or physical health, it's time to cut our losses and move on to another department or company. And by "we" I mean not only employees at the bottom of the chain, but also managers. There is a good chance that the crazy-maker coworker who is driving you nuts is having the same effect on management.

Speaking of management: in a break with long-standing techie tradition, and a breach of techie etiquette that will undoubtedly earn me the odium of fellow bottom-dwellers, I will also include, where possible, the management point of view. It is a cherished fantasy among people being forced to deal with difficult coworkers or situations that management could, if they wanted to, fix these things — that nothing but a lack of understanding or will is what stops them from resolving issues.

In talks over the years with managers willing to risk

discussing things openly, I've gained some perspective on how things happen at their level. With an understanding of the limitations placed on what steps they can take to deal with even the most disruptive behavior, the stereotype of the manager as hapless idiot has gotten to seem less true in general.

Straitjacketed by fear of lawsuits, managers must consult human resources and legal departments before even the most minor disciplinary actions are considered. And although it would be nice, "I'm annoyed" or "I'm offended" are not legal standards, and a lot of things that are seriously irritating are not, in the current parlance, "actionable." That music you hear in the background is my fellow tech support serfs playing the Stones' old hit, "Sympathy For The Devil" while joining hands and preparing to shun me.

This is not a book that will offer tips on how to dazzle your coworkers, rise in the organization, make the world sit up and take notice, earn millions, or find inner peace. For facile platitudes and meaningless clichés go stand in a grocery store checkout line and scan the magazines, which now offer career advice along with can't-miss diets and the latest celebrity gossip.

This is more of a survival guide for those of us who will spend our working lives in positions of relative powerlessness, hoping to fit in, stay employed, avoid drama, and survive each day without long-term psychological damage.

Knowing when to wait out difficult circumstances, ignore bad advice, take good advice, and recognize absolute no-win situations are the coping strategies that have kept me employed. I'm also a big fan of creative solutions. My two favorites are the "stunt purse" trick as a way to deal with the incessant talkers described in "The Verbal Diarrhea Twins" and the secret behind my ascendency to project manager status in the look at expatriate communities. These are my masterpieces.

This is also not a book about pushing back or filing complaints, even in the face of situations where those things are clearly justified. My experience has been that bringing harassment or discrimination to the attention of management and expecting a remedy is likely to have a boomerang effect, marking the complainer with a sort of "third rail" aura.

In an industry that is notoriously non-tenurial being able to move between departments and get hired at new companies is critical, and all it takes is one former coworker letting a potential manager know that you filed a complaint to scotch a job offer.

On the few occasions when the harassment has gotten too bad to stand, I've dealt with it by relocating and leaving the irritation behind. The lessons gleaned from former coworkers who actually brought complaints and wound up with scant prospects the next time finding a new job became necessary have led me to believe that the old saying, "Better a live chicken than a dead duck" is as true in high-tech as in a barnyard.

As well as recognizing what other people do that can drive us crazy, it's also good once in a while to stop and think about what we do that causes gnashing teeth and raised blood pressure in the people around us. Everyone brings their personality to work with them, not just the people who are driving *you* bats.

So, as we look at the fellow inhabitants of our workspaces, keep this in mind: with a bit of self-awareness, most of us will be able to find something about ourselves that looks familiar among the denizens of **The Office Zoo.**

The Bachelor Herd

A couple of years ago I went on vacation to a wildlife park in Northern California. The jeep containing my tour group bumped along dirt roads past the giraffes, zebras and assorted other animals for a while then stopped by a herd of some kind of cattle-like grazers. After giving us a bit of general information about this herd, the guide pointed out that there was only one male in the group, and told us why. This lucky beast was the winner of the annual horn-bashing contest these animals engage in to decide who gets all the girls, and was now contentedly enjoying his "harem" of ten or so females.

After males in the herd slugged it out for breeding rights for the year the losers, those poor defeated wimps, along with boy cattle too young to even compete, had to leave the herd. Their lot was to slink off to lick their wounds and take up residence elsewhere, while the male we were looking at now got to enjoy a happy mating-season-long bovine boinkfest and a crop of calves with his cute nose and dominant-male DNA.

On the way back to the tents, we rounded a curve, and there they were: the bachelor herd. Looking as disgruntled as animals with an extremely limited range of facial expressions can, this lonely pack huddled together under a few trees. No dates and zero prospect of any social life involving the opposite sex until next mating season, when they could try again. Being non-human they unfortunately had no Xbox, sports channel, take-out pizza or games of golf with each other to help pass the time. Not having language, they couldn't engage in any sour-grapes excuses to explain their failures: the winner was juicing, had undergone horn enhancement surgery, could afford a better coach. Our guide pointed out how stoically they accepted their fate, refraining from challenging the winner to a rematch and staying well away from the grazing territory now occupied by this year's victor and his lady friends.

Back at work on Monday, mind still on my brief vacation, I wandered over to the open area containing the test and development staff to find a friend and get caught up on anything interesting that might have happened while I was gone. Gazing out from the top of a stairway something suddenly looked interesting in the cubes below me in a slightly different way than it usually did. Then it clicked. I was looking at a human version of the bachelor herd.

As is true in many high-tech companies almost all of the occupants in the test and development departments were male. I'd been there long enough to know a lot of them fairly well, and that was probably why they reminded me so much of the poor also-rans commiserating with each other under the trees. The social prospects for many of the guys hunched over their laptops were, sadly, very similar to their brethren in the wildlife park.

Like the bachelor herd, many of them had no regular dates. They may not have had an absolute zero chance of any prospect for a social life involving the opposite sex, but close to it. Although the social rituals they were required to engage in to compete for mates didn't exactly, literally, involve bashing heads with other males, the human version of those rituals were, even so, contests in which these guys generally failed. Many had tried repeatedly for female companionship and lost out to what women considered to be more appealing males. In conversations I'd had with some of them about their attempts at socializing, they'd looked about as unhappy as creatures with a somewhat limited range of facial expressions can.

Unlike the bachelor herd, however, these unattached males could try to line up dates without having to wait a year after each failure. Many did, accessing online dating services, joining groups that arranged social activities for single people, and hanging out where other unattached people were likely to go. Yet most were still flying solo and spent weekends with each other, alone, or at work. Why was this?

Part of the problem is that in the era of speed-dating and online matchmaking, an instant good first impression based on either a picture and brief biography or a few sweaty, nerve-wracking minutes of face-to-face time with potential partners on a coffee or lunch date is critical. Unfortunately, many members of this techie bachelor herd have a serious lack of both curb appeal and social skills.

Increasingly suffering from the same issues about appearance that women have been dealing with approximately forever, the short, slightly overweight programmer is likely to lose out to the photogenic guy with six-pack abs and cute dimples. My coworkers just don't show as well as the competition. Being around members of the human bachelor herd long enough to appreciate their good points might require a degree of patience and tolerance not really necessary when there are so many other potential dates in your Match.com inbox.

This is unfortunate because, at least in my opinion, a number of these strays would probably make good husbands and fathers even though they may not be particularly exciting dates. Getting someone to go out with them in the first place and hang in long enough to get past some initial shyness and diffidence is difficult. They tend to be direct in ways that put them at a disadvantage in understanding the artifices often called for in dating.

Someone who admits that long sunset walks on the beach just seem to involve a bunch of uncomfortable sand in your shoes and a chance to catch a chill, and who suffers from "museum feet" after ten minutes of tapestry-gazing may not make the cut even if Mr. Cute Dimples is lying when he claims to love the feel of seaweed between his toes and, he claims, wouldn't miss that Caravaggio exhibit for the world. Looking at the bios of these two potential dates, as well as a dozen others that purport to be excellent cooks, hopeless romantics, half-marathoners and pet lovers, it's understandable that my coworkers barely rate a civil turndown from the women they have expressed an interest in.

Which brings up another aspect of dating in Silicon Valley: an imbalance in numbers. With more single men than women, it's a "buyer's market" for the women, although I've heard complaints from girlfriends about winnowing through first dates with men who, from their description, could easily be the guys in the cubes around me. As one girlfriend pointed out, "the odds are good, but the goods are odd." Other parts of the country undoubtedly have their own imbalances, as the constant stream of articles in national magazines about the difficulty single women face in rounding up dates indicate. Maybe the possibility of an exchange program between Silicon Valley and some of these areas should be explored.

What my girlfriends lamenting the oddness of the "goods" can't see when reading that bio or going on a first date with these unprepossessing geeks are things I've gotten to know over time.

Gaining a good close look at them has been a lot easier for me than for my single friends since I'm part of their daily landscape. Working closely with someone every day gives you much more accurate information about them than the superficial impression gleaned from a few lunches and movies.

Being married and therefore not any kind of potential social connection, I don't inspire the tongue-tied bungling which is the first, and sometimes only, thing their dates see before moving on to the next possibility. As one of them pointed out to me, "It's easy to talk to you about things — you aren't really a girl." Even though his choice of words was a bit unfortunate, I understood what he meant. Without the overlay of tension accompanying the "interview" atmosphere of dating, it was possible to be relaxed and open, not to mention a bit more coherent.

Even given the relatively poor optics of my coworkers compared to the dimples-and-rockhard-abs crowd, I still think that someone out there is missing out on a good bet by being so quick to turn down the guy with coke-bottle glasses. Getting to know him a bit better might reveal someone who routinely deals with setbacks gracefully, tackles difficult or distasteful work without complaining, holds his temper when a coworker accidentally trashes a test setup that took a week to build, and volunteers to help coworkers even when it means staying late or coming in on a weekend — all great indicators in the search for husband material.

The innate tension of one-on-one social occasions like first dates can make anyone clumsy. I've sat through a number of regret-filled Monday-morning recitations of what would have been a better thing to say or do. Pointing out that first-date nerves are something even the most socially adept can experience really doesn't help. If there is anyone out there who has never said something inappropriate or stupid in a tense social situation, please raise your hand.

Hmmmm...no hands? Not surprising.

Other complications common to both the socially awkward and everyone else are the cumulative aftereffects of previous romances, whether they included marriage or not. Other than people who marry way early and never look back, most people have a few psychological dings in their hide and other possible complications resulting from past relationships. This is one of the things that can make the dating aftermarket so difficult for everyone. Dealing with things like a suspicious streak caused by a former partner's infidelity or lying, children whose needs have to be put first, or trouble stirred up by an ex who hasn't quite let go even after the divorce is final can be trying for anyone. But for the acres of introverts I've worked with they can be impossible.

For all of these reasons, the human bachelor herd will probably always be around, even though so many of them would do well in stable long-term relationships. Their persistence in continuing the search for companionship is impressive, since after a certain number of turndowns and short, unsuccessful relationships, they approach new possibilities with a constantly shifting mix of emotions, hopeful and cautious at the same time. At least the herd of cattle exiled from the territory occupied by the alpha horn-basher and his harem only has to deal with a turndown once a year, which might, come to think of it, be easier than getting rejections in your inbox every week.

For anyone reading this who may now be thinking about that software engineer who seemed too awkward to continue seeing consider this: my own experience proves that this band of unmarried brothers is worth looking at more closely. I am married to a former member of the bachelor herd, and what is true for my current coworkers was true of him. He was not a particularly sparkling first date but has been a wonderful husband for many years.

The Enforcer

By now, everyone knows the dangers of smoking: lung problems, a panoply of other health issues, secondhand smoke affecting anyone in the vicinity, yellow teeth and a heavy dose of social disapproval. But even the American Lung Association couldn't have foreseen this one: out in the cube farm, lying in wait was a self-appointed watcher, a human monitor observing the smokers each time they went out, carefully tracking how long and how frequently they were gone. Martina kept notes, and frequently mentioned how much the smokers were away from their desks. Didn't management know, she would ask, how much less work than non-smokers they must be doing? Tactfully agreeing with her each time she asked this question, I avoided pointing out that management must know, since she had informed them a number of times.

If "smoker patrol" was the extent of Martina's watchfulness, most of us wouldn't have minded. Smokers are an easy and acceptable target for general disdain, one of the few and constantly dwindling number of groups left where being judgmental is ok. They feel like pariahs anyway, and are already two-thirds of the way toward feeling guilty about their habit.

But that was nowhere near where Martina's vigilance stopped. Being a model watchdog, she also kept an eye on: bathroom breaks, snack breaks, time spent in conversation in the aisles between cubes, and what she called "personal call" time — occasions when we wanted some privacy for a phone call. We'd grab our cell phones and head out to a corridor or the parking lot to make calls out of earshot of coworkers. The time between departure from and arrival back at our cubes would be carefully tallied.

An errand that involved being out of the building during the day? Martina would record the time left and the time returned. An auditing firm would appreciate the precision with which Martina tracked our activities, a degree of accuracy that could only have been surpassed by having a chip implanted in coworkers with a tracking application to monitor our movements.

The only metric not counted up and remarked on was the amount of time Martina spent monitoring other people's activities. If it weren't for the near certainty that it would only make matters worse, we were tempted to ask the person in the cubicle next to her to track how much time she spent checking up on other employees, and mention it during her next recitation of how much so-and-so was away from their desk each week. However, as is common with self-appointed authoritarians, Martina was somewhat humorless and, we thought, likely to be offended by a move like that. She was a prime example of someone who can dish it out but can't take it. Also, it seemed unlikely that she would get the point, so we decided not to try.

In addition to her role as our timekeeper, Martina had also nominated herself to be the enforcer of rules. Badge not openly displayed between shoulder and hip? Food left in the refrigerator on Friday night? Paper not disposed of in the correct recycling bin? She had an amazing talent for always being close by to record and point out any infraction, no matter how small. Her detailed knowledge of material in the phonebook-sized employee guidelines manual was a tribute to her ability to plow through fine print and arcane language. Like many governance documents it contained verbiage so dry and boring that its optimal use would have been as a doorstop — or a cure for insomnia.

To their credit, on occasions when Martina confronted managers, both her own and others', with a compendium of petty sins committed by her coworkers, they generally listened politely, took whatever documentation she provided, and agreed that they would "take it under consideration" or "take whatever action" was deemed necessary — and then did nothing.

She was a generally good worker, handing in assignments on time and holding up her end of the workload. Beyond being a bit irritating, she was not that difficult to deal with, answering work-related questions efficiently when asked, getting help from coworkers when she needed it, and participating in meetings without going off on a tangent too often about the deficits of other people's work habits. She was actually a pretty good team player, but her constant alertness about even the smallest and most innocuous infractions could fray our nerves.

Even though Martina wasn't that difficult to put up with there are a few problems with self-appointed monitors. Occasionally someone like Martina winds up in a job with some actual authority. As a peer, she could only annoy us. However, one year we wound up with a corporate compliance officer who made Martina look like a model of easygoing tolerance. Printouts not picked up within thirty minutes? An email would be sent to our manager, describing the infraction. Second offense? Second-level manager notified. Eventually, as the alerts were being issued by someone with a bit of actual power, repeated lag times in picking up printouts could wind up affecting reviews and raises.

Dealing with Martina was annoying in the way that any type of constant observation and monitoring can be. As noted in the introduction to this book, she was a part of the cubescape people tried to avoid, going to great lengths to stay off her list of offenders even though management didn't generally take her seriously.

In the movie "Nine to Five" the office fink, Roz, hides in a bathroom stall, feet tucked up to avoid detection, in order to eavesdrop on other employees. Thinking they have some privacy, two coworkers discuss an issue which Roz picks up and gleefully relays to management. Bearing that possible tactic in mind, people were careful about what they said in the restrooms or the break room, and this constant guardedness was wearing. Managers pressed for time disliked her visits, generally consisting of twenty or thirty minutes of tattle tales. She was smart enough not to rat out managers, although they also were undoubtedly watched.

There were a couple of positive things that grew out of having Martina around. As often happens when dealing with someone unilaterally trying to assert authority over peers, people teamed up to cope with her, providing an interesting "bonding" experience. As many political consultants and psychologists know, nothing makes people work together better than a common enemy. By alienating people so consistently, Martina had assumed that role.

This situation probably wasn't what the company had in mind as they constantly urged us to cooperate and work as a team to resolve issues, but for us this was an issue, and we were dealing with it by working as a team. Martina served as an interesting conversation piece, providing material for speculation about who was at the top of her list of malingerers when things were slow and there wasn't much else to talk about. We found creative ways to dispatch her to irrelevant meetings, send her to other floors to check with someone about something, or ask her to run out to the computer floor to inventory equipment just to get her out of the way for a few hours at a time.

A similar method of circumventing mindless authoritarianism had actually provided a great benefit for me early in my career. The company I worked for at the time had a site manager who was a "Martina" clone promoted to a level of authority that far exceeded his level of common sense. He had implemented a "late book" program which required employees who came in after the official 8:00 am start time to sign in and explain their tardiness, kicking off a string of communications that required managers to respond with acknowledgements and expressions of our regret about violating site policy.

Since the "late book" only required signing in until 9:00 am, when it was assumed we were late due to returning from meetings in other buildings, most managers simply told us to go hang out at the local coffee shop until then to avoid the paperwork on days when we came in late. By doing this we avoided being put on report, and managers didn't have to deal with annoying communications, although they did lose an hour of our work.

Owing to the occasional late night or traffic tie-up, I wound up at the "truants table" once in a while. Chatting with the other scofflaws, I got to know people in different departments and made some useful contacts. Eventually one of these led to an internal transfer to a much better job. Another truant turned out to be someone I had a great deal in common with, and is a friend to this day.

As pretty much everyone in the environment knew about

Martina, we didn't take her too seriously. However, in years to come, the self-appointed watchers and enforcers of Martina's day would be replaced with technologies that are much more pervasive and difficult to cope with.

The advent of computer-based metrics to measure everything from keystrokes per hour to task start and completion times and breaks away from the keyboard means that email can be instantly and automatically dispatched about even the most minor violations. These communications are kicked off about infractions regardless of circumstances which might have made them either unavoidable or the better of two choices.

A friend who works as a phone advice nurse for a large health care provider once had a job where calls were tracked by a monitoring system programmed to regard any call over a certain number of minutes as excessively long. Anyone going over that limit could be required to provide an explanation to a supervisor about her tardiness in completing the call. Knowing that any advice nurse helping me in the future may have one eye on the clock, I will make every effort to have easily described and diagnosable issues.

The automation replacing Martina is now so widespread that even the most trivial aspects of employment are being monitored. At another company I worked for, one of the online programs tracked the use of an "employee appreciation" gift program. Employees could sign on to the site and give someone in another department an award for things like excellent service, good ideas, or outstanding effort on a project. Awards made this way were redeemable for an item from a catalog of trinkets. What was somehow not caught by the automated program was that, although there was a yearly limit of three such awards per recipient, the program did not stop a fourth award from being given. It did, however, stop the recipient from redeeming it, generating a message that the yearly limit of three awards could not be exceeded. The unredeemed award was regarded by the automated employee tracking system as an incomplete administrative task.

During my first ten months at the company I received three awards from satisfied customers. Each time, I carefully logged into the awards site and chose a trinket within the two-week window for processing the award, thereby clearing my queue of the administrative task.

But before my first calendar year of employment was reached another user, pleased with my weekend-long effort to bring a critical project back on schedule, nominated me for a fourth award. When I tried to redeem the award, the program rejected my attempt.

However, the unredeemed award stayed in my work queue. I could not figure out how to clear it and neither could my manager, who was also new to the company and unfamiliar with how to override or cancel administrative task violations. Understandably, this was low on his priority list as he thrashed through other unfamiliar tasks which were more urgent.

But when the two-week limit was reached emails began spewing forth from the program, alerting us both to my failure to address the matter, threatening to communicate with authorities higher up the food chain, and detailing the list of dire consequences which could result from failing to complete the pending task. The death penalty, thankfully, was not among the potential punishments but pretty much everything else was. I sent a string of increasingly frantic emails to my manager, contemplated whether or not to start carrying around enough cash to make bail if necessary, and tried to figure out if my résumé writing skills were creative enough to explain a job termination due to noncompliance with a trinket reward program.

After some time on the phone to the gift program

administrator, the manager was finally able to cancel the award and absolve me of wrongdoing, which was important since with a certain number of violations raises and promotions would be affected.

To the relief of overachieving employees throughout the company, the trinket award program was discontinued during the next economic downturn.

Although I never thought it would come to this, these days I'm nostalgic for the Martina years. Compared to dealing with the automated programs of today, which cannot be ignored, avoided, made fun of, or dispatched on made-up errands, the relatively minor annoyances of dealing with the self-appointed watcher seem trivial in retrospect. And all those times we wished she was gone? Guess we should have been careful what we wished for.

The Village Idiot

···

If the suggestion had been made by anyone else, we probably would have jumped on it. Evaluated on its own merit, without having come from someone the rest of us in the room regarded as the village idiot, it made sense. However, this was not the case. Sometimes the old saying "consider the source" is a good idea but sometimes, well, maybe not.

Faced with the need to upgrade and restructure a set of application servers the company was rapidly outgrowing, the team in the room was kicking around ideas. Split them up by department? Dedicate servers for applications and let groups share them? Time to look at the cloud? How would billing be handled? What about support issues?

Then, Harold — who pretty much everyone thought wouldn't have anything substantial to contribute to the discussion — suggested an approach that had the force of careful and reasonable logic behind it. There was abundant performance data, he reminded us, and if we went back and analyzed the last few months of that data and talked to department heads about what was ahead, we could probably come up with a usage profile that would be a good starting point for the reconfiguration.

Silence. Then Jason, who often led the charge as Harold's biggest critic, and whose mouth was often a step or two ahead of his brain, jumped in with "That's an irrelevant approach because...", and then there was a pause while he tried to come up with a reason to regard Harold's suggestion as useless. We all waited, glad not to have responded without thinking it through.

The role of "Village Idiot" in a workplace — or a class, a town, a family, or a social group — is an interesting one. It can be conferred by someone in the group with enough stature to get everyone else to go along. It can be earned by diligent effort, or lack of effort. It can be stumbled into through an inadvertent error in the first few days on the job, one clumsy moment when meeting people for the first time, a misunderstanding about social norms in a new environment, or sudden reassignment to completely unfamiliar work projects.

The upside of having a Village Idiot is that it can provide a convenient way for other group members to feel smug and superior about their own skill level or social standing. The downside is the automatic attachment of "Village Idiot Cooties" to any suggestions coming from the occupant of this role — as had just happened in the architecture meeting. Following the awkward pause, Jason had come up with an obscure reason to dismiss Harold's input, and the conversation moved on.

Although I hadn't worked with either Jason or Harold much, after noticing that no one else spoke up in favor of Harold's suggestion I kept quiet also, curious about what had happened to make Harold so toxic that anything he said was automatically regarded as not worth consideration.

The next time I ran into Harold I struck up a casual conversation. How long had he been in the architecture group?

Where had he worked before that?

After a few minutes the background of Harold's trajectory into Village Idiot status became clear. In the last corporate reorganization his former position had been cut when the company dumped the project he was working on. In an effort to resettle employees inside the company instead of laying them off, he had been offered a position in the architecture group. His new job would require a completely different set of skills then his old one. By Harold's own admission he was, at least initially, completely unqualified for his new job. Another part of the same reorganization that had landed Harold in a new group had sliced out training money, and the company was no longer willing to pay for classes that had previously been available to new employees in the department.

However, grateful to still be employed, Harold took the job and spent his first six months searching the internet for information, leaning on already-overburdened coworkers for help, paying for a few courses with his own money, and trying to make himself useful in his new department in any way he could.

Unfortunately Jason, one of Harold's new coworkers, was both prone to making snap judgments about people and resistant to changing his opinions about pretty much anything once they were formed. He was also rather vocal about his thoughts. Jason's quick pronouncement of Harold as slow, incompetent, and hopeless was picked up by the group, and presto — instant Village Idiot.

As often happens when the title is awarded, there was a recursive downward cycle of effects. Coworkers were impatient with Harold when he needed help, and as dismissive of his suggestions as Jason was. When Harold had come up to speed on the technical aspects of his job and developed a good level of expertise, other people avoided asking for his help. Who wants to be seen asking the Village Idiot for assistance?

With a better understanding of how the situation had taken shape and an appreciation of the undercurrents between Harold and the rest of the group, I decided to go ahead and start mining historical performance data and talk to department heads about plans for the next year. Needless to say, this didn't go over too well with Jason or anyone else, but did yield some information that was ultimately useful in figuring out how to proceed.

Although Harold's current existence in "grin and bear it" mode had to have been uncomfortable, compared to other people I've seen assigned the Village Idiot label for one reason or another he actually seemed to be dealing with it fairly well.

In the same way that people can be spurred on to excellent work by knowing that the people around them have high expectations, the reverse is also true. Other people I'd seen going through the same thing had responded to facing a wall of negative opinions by simply withdrawing, and spiraling downward into mediocre performance. Harold's steadiness was impressive and, I had to admit, he was doing a much better job of coping than I had when what looked like a promising job change catapulted me into a similar situation.

My own turn as the Village Idiot came by way of some exhausted stumbling around in the first few weeks of a new job. The storage device I had been hired to work on was similar to ones I'd been involved in testing before, but would require some learning curve before I could get started. However, within a week my new manager, under pressure because of missed project deadlines, became furious at how long it was taking me to come up to speed on the new device.

His insistence that with my background I should easily be able to complete a test schedule that had project due dates going back to a month before I was hired became a constant point of contention. The fragmented, confusing and incomplete "onboarding" process left me wandering around the department for a few months begging annoyed coworkers to log me into systems I needed access to but hadn't yet been authorized for, and to walk me through test procedures that weren't documented anywhere.

As I became increasingly exhausted trying to meet the test schedule by working longer and longer days I began to make stupid, trivial mistakes, and wound up with a reputation as incompetent. Disoriented by operating on just a few hours of sleep a night for weeks on end nothing made sense, and I had to read even the most basic material several times before comprehending it.

With cause and effect chasing each other around in a circle I continued to struggle, and failed to meet the updated set of deadlines. I became insecure and began second-guessing myself over even the smallest decisions. Highly regarded at the company I had quit for my current one, the situation was humiliating. I became hesitant about asking coworkers for help or input. Was what I was about to ask a stupid question? Had it been covered in one of the thousands of emails I'd received in the last few weeks, possibly buried in one of the forwarded chains dozens of emails deep?

By the time I found my feet and began to complete work and hit schedules, it was too late. Opinion about me has ossified, and my role as the Village Idiot was cast in stone.

When it became clear that things wouldn't change, I managed to find a few ways to survive my place at the bottom of the pecking order. First, I simply accepted that this was the way things were going to be, and gave up worrying about it. Once past that, I started concentrating on working defensively. Extensive documentation was collected backing up each decision, and test results were buttressed by logs, narratives on the background of how each decision was made, and references to similar tests architected by respected group members.

Constantly worried about layoffs, I wasn't really playing to win — I was playing not to lose, trying to turn myself into a difficult target if layoffs were going to be based on performance. The write-ups of my test results were absolutely pristine, offering no chance for carping on either procedural grounds or on conclusions.

Second, I quietly began finding ways to contribute to group projects, volunteering for the universally-disliked committee work when someone in the group had to participate. Boring as it was to sit through earthquake preparedness drills and attend site safety meetings, on some level these things made an impact. Although opinions about me never really changed, after about six months my manager stopped complaining about me to anyone who would listen. It was an uneasy détente, definitely not an ideal situation but at least tolerable.

Although the existence of a Village Idiot in a group is so common, there are a couple of unfortunate aspects both for the person tagged for this, and for everyone else. Being in this role is degrading and uncomfortable. When someone like Harold winds up filling the spot, pushing back is difficult, both for Harold and for other group members. Speaking up for Harold would risk backlash from Jason, who was the dominant personality in the group. As often happens, the combination of one very strongly opinionated person in a group of "sheeple" had fostered this situation. Groups with a better overall degree of maturity and perspective don't really need someone to use as a human target for derision.

Also, as had happened at the architecture meeting, when everyone is spring-loaded to regard any input from the Village Idiot as worthless, truly useful suggestions might get passed by. Once minds are made up, it's difficult to coax people into reevaluating their thinking. In the same way that prejudices are clung to long after they should have been discarded, even after the usefulness of Harold's suggestion became abundantly clear opinion about him didn't seem to budge.

My own turn as the Village Idiot had been an eye-opening and painful experience. However, like a lot of painful experiences, by going through it I gained some perspective. Although "consider the source" fell into the maybe-not-a-good-idea this time, another old saying is absolutely true: there is nothing quite like having walked a few miles in those shoes to understand what it's really like.

The Human Tape Player

The sad, heartbreaking, emotional story was told with great feeling. Fred's family had been prosperous and well-known, moving in the best social circles. They were successful professionals, great donors to charity, involved with local schools Then a combination of layoffs, ill health, investments that turned bad and a deteriorating job market that reduced chances for reemployment had decimated the family fortunes. Now here they were, much poorer, working at jobs they would have scorned before, struggling, their circumstances severely reduced. It was a narrative fit for the annual flood of Christmas stories designed to spur charitable giving carried by newspapers around the country.

So why was I unmoved by this tale? Because it was at least the twentieth time I'd heard it. When Fred first told me about this, I was genuinely touched. The second time, hearing the same story repeated word for word, I wondered if there was a memory issue. Did he recall telling me this before? The third, fourth, and fifth times he launched the verbal family history "tape" I tried interrupting. The interruption had no effect — he merely continued. On subsequent occasions when he launched the tape, I turned to my laptop and starting to type and view email. He ignored these nonverbal cues and continued to the end of the tape, unruffled by my lack of attention. To the casual observer, I would have appeared callous. Who could treat someone relating the story of his family's misfortune that dismissively?

Gradually I noticed that Fred's tape was being played not only for me, but for numerous other people as well. Any conversation, no matter how trivial, could lead to a launch of the tape, repeated verbatim, same inflection, hand gestures and facial expressions, like an actor in a play running through the same performance, again and again.

The tape took about five minutes, and attempts to break in were either completely ignored or, worse, caused a reset to the beginning and a relaunch. After a certain number of iterations, most people had started to deal with this the same way I did — work on something else while waiting him out, leaving Fred talking happily and unconcernedly to air while finishing.

After the tape completed, Fred was able to move on and discuss other issues, so it had simply become an accepted thing — five minutes was really not that much, particularly if you could multitask. As coworkers often do, Fred had "trained" us in how to deal with him.

Who hasn't had to deal with a human tape player? Most of the time it's something innocuous: "Did I ever tell you about the time..." or "That reminds me of..."

However, some years ago I worked with a woman who replayed, endlessly and in minute detail, her experience during a barium enema. The launch of Lisa's tape could be triggered by anything, and aimed at anyone. She would accost people at the water fountain, on the way to or from the break room, while walking into the building together and, most annoyingly, at lunch.

Faced with the possibility of being subjected to a tape that people found a bit disgusting, we came up with a variety of ways to avoid Lisa. She was watched carefully: had she just taken her break and returned to her desk? Great time for everyone else to take theirs, knowing the coast was clear. Did she tend to come in through a side door by a certain parking lot? The other side of the building was suddenly a much more popular place to park. Was she headed this way? Time to put on the telephone headset and appear to be occupied. When caught in a launch of Lisa's tape, it was challenging to suddenly find a need to be somewhere else before she got to the part of the story about the hoses. Fred's recital of his family history looked positively attractive by comparison.

Although Fred and Lisa had tapes which were personal some types of issues, most notably politics, seem to be consistently popular. Political "tape players" subject coworkers to a constant stream of heartfelt invective about the bastards in office, the country's downhill slide, and the laziness and stupidity of today's youth — most of whom are currently headed for hell in a handbasket because they are just too damn lazy to walk there on their own two feet. The political "tapes" do have the advantage of varying slightly as fresh outrages are perpetrated, but they are just as unavoidable and uninterruptible as Fred and Lisa's tapes.

What causes people to fasten onto a story about their past, a particular experience, something that annoys them, an amusing incident — at least amusing the first time or two you hear it — and replay it endlessly? It's a mystery to me both why it happens and why human tape players avoid all efforts to short-circuit the hundredth retelling.

Although various efforts to stop Fred from playing his tape failed, it did become a source of amusement when, after realizing that it would be pointless to actually try to deal with, we started to count how often Fred played his "tape" for each of us and compare numbers at the end of the week. Although no actual prize was given for the highest number of times each of us was an unwilling audience, the more competitive among us began to actually bait Fred into playing the tape in order to win the weekly comparison. It was, at least, cheap entertainment for Friday afternoons. The twin megrims caused by boredom and confinement have given rise to far less innocuous games.

One benefit of having a "human tape player" to deal with was that it made me conscious of repeating things to other people. I began to be careful: had I mentioned the same story or instructions, or asked the same questions to this person before? People in the tape player comparison pool would catch themselves repeating things, laugh, and say "Uh oh — a Fred moment!"

We agreed that developing tolerance for this would help us eventually when parents, friends, or spouses developed memory issues, or during those tedious holiday gatherings when family legends were trotted out for the umpteenth time by a tipsy uncle. The strategy we used at work — smiling, waiting it out, logging occurrences — have turned out to be useful. Although I have run into a number of tape players in the years since I worked with Fred, I often remember him fondly during another endless repetition of a childhood story at Thanksgiving or Christmas.

To be fair there are times when launching a time-worn story at family reunions — or an office — is a welcome attempt to end an awkward silence or reroute a conversational path that seems to be leading to something unpleasant. When that same uncle is heading for a discussion on why a nephew somehow can't manage to find a job after all this time, the details of a family member's messy divorce, or the drug problem one of his kids has developed, interrupting with another recitation of the really cute thing Lizzie did when she was a baby seems like a great alternative.

And Fred? Last seen, he was still happily playing his tape for coworkers. He is undoubtedly retired by now, and I hope that the new social circles of retirement have provided him with fresh audiences as he continues to repeat his family saga.

The Help Vampire
— and Other 'Passengers'

It was the strangest thing. There were a number of people in Erin's group with about the same setup on their computers — applications, file shares, programs, access authorization levels — but for some reason Erin frequently had a serious issue that required immediate assistance, an issue which, she insisted, blocked her from doing any work until fixed.

New to the company about a year ago, as her workload had ramped up so had the number of problems she encountered. Over time Erin became a "frequent flier," familiar to everyone in the surrounding support organizations and a thorn in the side of her coworkers.

The story was always the same. She was completely stuck until we: restored copies of her files from six weeks ago (before she made all those incorrect changes) figured out why her laptop was so slow, showed her (again) how to access files, launch programs, make updates. We reset her password. Help tickets rolled in, both for issues involving the local support staff, and for the remote help desk in Bangalore.

Looking back over tickets filed by her division one quarter, we found that she was using more of the support staff's time than the rest of her department put together. And that was just the staff outside her group, where the amount of time she was taking up could be tracked. Her coworkers did not have clear metrics showing how much of their time she was chewing up, but were clearly under some stress and running out of patience.

After the first few months of dealing with Erin, the people in her group had begun to refuse her efforts to engage them, realizing that giving in to her requests for "just a few minutes" or "some help with one thing" would be like agreeing to put one toe into quicksand, an engagement that was likely to result in being sucked into what might turn out to be hours of aggravation. They, at least, had the option of telling her to fill out a help ticket for her problem du jour. The support groups, including the one I was in, were not so lucky.

Erin was a "Help Vampire" — a creature who could drain time and energy from people around her with constant demands for assistance of one type or another. Like vampires everywhere, she needed a constant supply of new people. As each person tired of her endless requests and refused to work with her, she would simply move on to someone else.

Since the constant string of situations in which she could not, in her opinion, be held responsible for completing work until the cavalry was dispatched to rescue her continued, the support staff finally confronted her about this in a meeting with Erin and her manager. Explaining why these things "just happened," she simply claimed that although she was in a group of people doing work that was similar to hers there were aspects of this work which were unique to her assignments, and those unique — and uniquely difficult! — tasks were causing the problems.

Her hand-wringing and dramatic rendition of "…no one

knows how complicated it is to do what I do" was worthy of the most temperamental and talented diva, a melodic recitation fit for an Italian opera house. Although my self-restraint was sorely taxed, I did manage not to stand up and cheer after her closing lines. However, although the performance had been entertaining, no real progress was made in dealing with the issue, and the problems persisted.

Having dealt with a number of "Help Vampires" I have noticed an interesting characteristic they have in common. For some the real goal was to get constant attention or to annoy other people. However, for almost all of them, it was also a tactic to shift responsibility for pretty much everything to someone else.

Erin's real goal was to be a "passenger."

A "passenger" is someone who does not want to be responsible for part, or all, of what is either a shared responsibility or a responsibility which should be theirs alone. They wish to sit in the passenger side of the car, enjoying the view, while someone else does the driving, navigating, refueling and maintenance — and covers all expenses.

Viewed in this light, "Help Vampires" have a lot in common with other types of "passengers," not just at work, but in other areas of life.

Almost all relationships among people involve shared work or responsibility of some type: completing part of the preparations for an event, splitting the expenses, getting up in the middle of the night for diaper changes/feeding, enforcing consistent discipline with unruly teenagers, helping mom and dad, getting your part of the housework done.

"Passengers" duck out on their end of either implied or explicitly stated arrangements regarding who will do what, leaving all of the work to someone else. Ever had your name on the utility bill and wound up with a roommate who somehow never has the money to cover half? Financial passenger. The friend who's always happy to go along with plans other people make but never bothers to do any of the planning herself? Social passenger. Been in a group with someone like Erin? Work passenger.

So how did we wind up with her? In some ways, the initial stages of dating are similar to the initial stages of employment interviews. Although you can look for obvious no-go signals early on in the process, determining who will work out well in the long run is not so easy. While the forty-year-old who is crashing at his sister's house for two years while he is "between jobs," and who sells a little weed to raise cash can be passed up for further consideration, for employers it's a bit more difficult. Potential employees who will turn out to be work passengers (or have a number of other not-so-obvious deficits) can be hard to identify.

In the modern climate of caution regarding potential lawsuits, former employers generally supply nothing but employment dates, regardless of why an employee was let go — or quit ahead of being fired after a number of warnings. Former coworkers will generally say nothing negative if contacted by recruiters or hiring managers, avoiding even the slightest possibility of legal repercussions regarding libel or slander. Even the most unjustified legal action requires mounting a distracting and expensive defense, and people are understandably unwilling to risk having this happen to them.

Erin had done well during interviews. She had seemed personable, intelligent, and knowledgeable in her field. However, a strange kind of reverse alchemy had transformed her from shiny, promising prospect into inert stumbling block.

When it became clear that the constant requirements for support resources and coworkers' patience would not change, and because she was doing nothing her manager felt was egregious enough to warrant more serious job actions, most parts of her workload were gradually shifted to other employees.

They were, needless to say, less than delighted, but the work-onomics of having several extra tasks, balanced against having to either help Erin again or waste energy fending her off made this solution a relative bargain.

As her tasks became fewer and simpler, the help tickets dwindled somewhat and became easier to deal with. Her password could be reset for the nth time, her system rebooted, her questions answered with almost no effort. Relieved of the responsibility for making updates to critical files, her frequent requests to restore previous versions of those files tapered off.

One of Erin's earlier tricks had been to launch an accusation that "something" had gotten screwed up when a database was offline for backup or upgrade. This would require someone else to do part of her work to demonstrate that no harm had been done during the outage. Her workload was now so narrow that her coworkers were freed from having to do this after overnight maintenance windows, and they stopped trying to come in late enough to avoid being the one asked to help her.

Eventually this situation was resolved. When the next reduction in force occurred, giving managers some leeway in deciding who to lay off, Erin was at the top of the list. She had managed to hang on for two years, about the same amount of time she had been with her previous company.

In retrospect, a pattern of jobs held for relatively short times might possibly have been a red flag, but she had good explanations for this: work offshored, company reorganized, projects cancelled.

Moving from job to job in short time frames is so common in Silicon Valley that it didn't stand out as being unusual. Other employees with the same history of short stints had worked out well and stayed for years.

Happily, at least for Erin, with references verifying her

dates of employment and nothing negative that could be shared with potential new employers, she was easily able to find another job.

Quietly throwing a party in the back of their minds when they heard she was leaving, her coworkers didn't mind splitting up the paltry tasks she had been working on when she was let go. For our part, after her termination paperwork had been completed, the support staff drew straws to determine who would have the pleasure of disabling her user accounts.

The Tyranny
of Instant Communication

The idea was almost within my grasp, close by yet somehow just out of reach. Like waking up from a dream and being unable to remember something that seemed important, it had been there, but now it was gone.

A few minutes ago, the answer to a tricky and elusive problem had been coming into focus, a way out of the maze I'd been stumbling around in. After months of working perfectly a user's application had suddenly refused to initialize, instead generating messages that were either obscure, meaningless, or misleading. After exhausting the Google possibilities and plowing through vendor manuals that had obviously been translated from Martian into Quasi-English by workers hired from the fringes of the local Home Depot parking lot (example: "if there is no program, then do not program"), I finally decided to go through the painstaking process of tracing the code initialization instruction by instruction. This had yielded a possibility about why it was no longer working. But then...

Suddenly a pulsating bubble leapt onto my screen, slapping me in the face and chasing the idea just far enough away to be unavailable. It was followed in quick succession by two more bubbles — slap! slap! — throbbing like the first one until they were acknowledged by moving the cursor to each one and clicking. I tried to return to the set of debugging screens but like the details of an interrupted dream the idea was gone and I was left staring at the instant communications sent by coworkers, insistently demanding attention.

Because of the number of distracting bubbles arriving each day (which, although annoying, were greatly exceeded by the number of daily emails) I had been coming in earlier and earlier to try to deal with issues that would benefit from an uninterrupted train of thought, trying to work them out before everyone else came in and started launching bubbles.

However, other people were getting wise to this and were either coming in earlier to work with me or sending their bubbles from home. I had tried shutting down the communicator program but this was an unsuccessful strategy. When I signed out other people could see that my system was online to the network but not signed in to the communicator program and sent emails wanting to know why, or worse, contacted someone who worked in the same area and sent them over to "remind" me to log in.

And what was it that was so critically important? The first message was a question about what I planned to bring to the potluck on Friday. I had signed up for dessert, but could I bring salad instead? Message two was a request for some details of a presentation I'd be giving in a week. Message number three wanted me to research a performance issue and report back — there was a meeting in thirty minutes, could I please process the data from that unexplained slowdown last week, generate a report, and have it emailed by then?

After dealing with the bubbles, I tried to reboard the train of thought but it had left the station, stranding me with the partially executed program. The trail was cold. Nothing left to do but look at the file I'd been creating of each line of code and the data listed out and start again. Irritating, since I'd been so close to the answer — before the bubbles.

In the short story "Harrison Bergeron," Kurt Vonnegut describes a society where anyone capable of sustained thought is required by law to have a "mental handicap" radio device implanted by the "Handicapper General." The device would send out sharp, distracting noises every twenty seconds to prevent any thoughts in progress from being completed. The reason for this was that since not all people were capable of deep and sustained thought, the absolutely level "mental playing field" mandated by a recent constitutional amendment now required that no one be allowed to engage in this type of thinking.

Although the year in which this story takes place is 2081 current technology, often way ahead of predictions made by science fiction, has demonstrated how prescient Vonnegut was. Today, many decades ahead of the year in which "Harrison Bergeron" takes place, instant communications programs have assumed the role of the Handicapper General's implanted devices, making sure that uninterrupted thought is close to impossible.

Before the various bubble programs linked us with everyone else on a network, dealing with two or three people who had requests in the same time frame had been easier in a couple of ways. If there were people waiting to talk to someone in a cube or office each of the people waiting could see the others, and either wait their turn for assistance or come back later. Faced with a delay in getting questions answered another possibility was to figure out solutions on their own, which happened an interestingly high percentage of the time. Unless they were willing to be unusually rude (or considered

their request to be urgent) people did not all talk simultane-
ously or interrupt. If person B did interrupt, generally person
A, although annoyed, would be forced to wait. But at least
person A and person B knew in real time that the other was
speaking.

Because each person sending a bubble is visually removed
from the person on the receiving end, it is a common illu-
sion among bubble senders that theirs is either the only or the
most important bubble that the recipient is dealing with. The
senders cannot see the other bubbles being dealt with simulta-
neously and expect replies very quickly — after all, why else
would they call it "instant" communication? Since anyone
on the network is listed as "online and available" unless they
inform the program that they want to be listed as unavailable,
the person filling out the list of who will bring what to the
potluck expects an immediate reply, unaware of the requests
to generate performance analysis numbers and send details of
next week's presentation.

A second way in which multiple requests for help in the
same time frame were easier before the bubble era was that
employees were not linked with networks that included
people in other buildings, cities, countries. With the advent
of all that impressive connectivity and those worldwide networks, on most days bubbles come in from a variety of time
zones and geographic locations.

Why not use email to request information about something happening a week from now? Because it is so difficult
to deal with the volume of email, which can run to hundreds of messages a day, requests like "what are you bringing
to the potluck?" may get buried under ten or twenty emails
within a short time and be ignored or forgotten after more
pressing subjects have been handled. But a bubble sitting right
on the screen is much harder to ignore. There are no good
ways to avoid the bubbles. Closing them without replying

is considered a breach of bubble etiquette, answering them breaks concentration, letting them hang there reproachfully waiting to be answered is an annoyance.

Some of the instant communicator programs have bubbles which do not automatically appear onscreen and slap the recipient, showing up instead on the task bar at the bottom of the screen and pulsing a few times before falling silent. After moving to a company with the quieter bubbles I was constantly late responding since they were so unobtrusive that they were easily missed, but I was getting a lot more work done.

Whether the slap or non-slap version of the bubbles are being dealt with, there are several positive aspects of instant communications. First, those long boring meetings can be made more interesting by taking the opportunity to chat with other bored attendees. Since people bring laptops to most meetings now, getting a seat against a wall or other location where your screen is not visible is important. Doing this also affords a chance to play an electronic version of "buzzword bingo," checking off predicted platitudes and phrases as they are uttered. This is a very "green" modification to the way the game had been played previously by eliminating the need for paper lists.

Second, similar to email, the bubbles create electronically stored transcripts of the conversation, which came in handy as a trail of exactly what was said. It would be hard for someone to claim they hadn't committed to sending information, completing a task or promising to bring salad instead of dessert when an electronic record of the conversation could be copied from the instant message logs and sent to jog the memory. This does have a down side, however. As the long string of disgraced politicians and rock stars illustrate, the stored transcripts can be dredged up and used in scandalous tabloid articles, messy divorce cases, and other legal actions.

It is strange that even with so many lurid public embarrassments caused by stored electronic communications records otherwise intelligent and careful public figures are still snared this way.

The third benefit of bubble communication is the most interesting. It has become increasingly common for emails requesting help or information to be handled by forwarding them to another person. Each person in the chain can claim that they "dealt with" the issue and were no longer responsible in any way by simply adding a note that Joe was the one who usually worked on whatever the email is asking, and forwarding it to Joe, carefully cc'ing everyone else so that they will then be waiting for Joe to respond. Joe could then point out that Sue had more experience and was more likely to know the answer, and send the mail on, also cc'ing everyone. Similar to the children's game of "Hot Potato," the goal is to get rid of the item as quickly as possible and make it someone else's problem. This tactic creates email chains that are often ten or fifteen forwarded emails deep, requiring recipients to read through the entire stack to get a picture of what is being asked.

Bubble communications have character limits similar to tweets, although somewhat larger. This means that bubbles have to be shorter and more concise, containing, at least initially, a direct question or stating a specific problem.

Like many new challenges ushered in by technical innovation, the bubbles are really just one part of the overall issue of too much interaction. On "trifecta" days — enough instant communications for a virtual bubble bath, coworkers standing in the cube waiting for some help, a ringing phone — the amount of actual work getting done is close to zero. Everyone has had a few days when the main reason nothing is getting done is that must-respond communications are arriving on a minute-by-minute basis, peremptorily demanding to know why nothing is getting done.

So what happened to my user with the program that suddenly refused to initialize? Sadly, he would have to wait until the next day, when I came in even earlier, for a resolution. Although I had tried getting back to my debugging once the first three bubbles were taken care of, by then the rest of the crew was in and I spent the rest of the day, when not in meetings, playing whack-a-mole with a new set of bubbles.

Software Shitheads

T his was such a familiar and predictable humiliation that
the only real question was why it bothered me so much
today. Okay, fine, I was willing to agree with Nelson: he
knew more about using this system than the rest of us. His
superior knowledge made him more important than anyone
else. We were all just hangers-on. He could undoubtedly
complete the entire project faster by himself than with the
rest of us "dragging him down" by being involved. We were
not fit to kiss the hem of his garments, which today consisted
of the usual grubby jeans and stained shirt. The ingrates in
management didn't appreciate the fact that if he left, the company would undoubtedly collapse. He could ruin everything
just by walking out!

To emphasize his point, Nelson had, as usual, just started
spouting a stream of technical jargon describing system inter-
nals that left everyone else scratching their heads. Even on
good days, the amount of petting, cosseting and salaaming
obeisance required to obtain Nelson's cooperation for even
the most minor task drained energy. But today, tired and a bit
out of sorts from dealing with other work that was not going

well, I was having trouble waiting out the self-aggrandize-
ment-and-posturing stage which Nelson always performed
as a prelude to actually supplying answers or assistance. The
amount of control required to keep nodding and agreeing
while I waited him out was monumental.

Most technical environments have at least one "Nelson."
The breeding grounds for these "Software Shitheads" exist
everywhere and consist of a combination of ingredients: technical specialties that are being covered by a limited number
of people (a software shithead prefers an area where he is the
sole proprietor), coworkers who depend on him for a critical
process or information, compliant management that either
doesn't bother with or can't afford cross-training or backup
for key areas, an employee with a runaway ego who will
actively block anyone else from encroaching on his "territory," and an environment that tolerates employees who will
not share passwords or allow anyone else a level of authorization which would let them develop expertise.

After dealing with a number of "Nelsons" I had begun
to include several factors in calculating what dealing with a
software shithead would involve, thinking of it as the "cost of
interaction," or the "cost of information retrieval." Getting
Nelson's help would involve X amount of time spent listening
to some ranting, Y amount of aggravation, and possibly Z
number of emails to his manager. At one point, insisting that
he needed to nap between meetings, Nelson demanded that
someone come to his office and wake him ten minutes before
meeting start times. Our manager meekly dealt with this by
dispatching one of us to complete this errand. Locked out of
any kind of access that would allow the rest of us to look at
run logs, analyze problems, and propose solutions, we were
totally dependent on Nelson for problem determination and
fix, and the manager was tiptoeing around him as carefully
as we were.

Further annoying everyone, in Nelson's opinion his extraordinary talents should have excused him from administrative work the rest of us were required to complete. Why did he have to file status reports, attend mandatory safety drills, sit through department meetings? Why was he being asked to provide documentation for tests that he claimed were completed? The rest of us idiots should just take his word that the tests were run and, he claimed, we probably wouldn't understand the documents he created anyway. Shuddering at the thought of what documentation produced by Nelson would look like, I had to agree with him there.

He regarded himself as an "artist" — didn't management understand that weighing him down with the petty and unrewarding work required of lesser mortals could harm his special brand of creativity? Efforts to get management to require that master passwords be shared with at least one other person, or that administrative access by someone else be allowed, had failed. Nelson would just threaten to walk out and they would back down, not wanting to risk upheaval. As things got worse, Nelson's manager chose to deal with this by moving on to another job, deciding to leave the situation for the next manager to deal with. Irritating as this transfer was, I had to admire the manager's talent for survival.

Several years ago a software shithead working on San Francisco's FibreWAN network, which was used for functions such as payroll and email, managed to be the only person with the master password. After being jailed for refusing to share it, he demanded a personal meeting with then-mayor Gavin Newsom as a condition for turning it over. Prior to that jailhouse meeting, he claimed that he was refusing the request because other city officials were "not qualified" to have network access.

An April 10, 2010 Network World article describing the incident included the observation that this engineer was somewhat "lacking in interpersonal skills." Really? Although the incident was dramatic and held public attention in San Francisco for some time, the real issue was the environment which set the stage for this to happen in the first place. The engineer was eventually convicted of network tampering and wound up spending some time in jail. However, he has the distinction of serving forever as a role model for software shit-heads everywhere.

Another reason that information technology is a fertile breeding ground for these oversized egos is that each job can be very specialized. Key employees are not easily replaced without the risk of potential disruption even in the best of circumstances. Network and database positions at the top of the technical food chain have a limited pool of poten-tial applicants, and it can take months for even a well-quali-fied employee to come up to speed in a new environment. In many departments, managers and coworkers are unlikely to understand the details of what a database or network specialist is doing, relying on some degree of maturity on the employ-ee's part to avoid situations like the one in San Francisco. But where that maturity is lacking, these factors can create the playgrounds in which software shitheads flourish.

What holds down the number of "Nelsons" in some vocations is the availability of alternatives. If your mechanic refused to work on your car until you sat through an hour-long discussion on the finer points of the internal combus-tion engine, agreeing every few minutes that yes, you are an idiot compared to him as far as knowledge of engines is con-cerned, you would find another mechanic. Every field has a number of arcane details and work-related jargon not familiar to outsiders. However, with a dry cleaner on every corner, it is unlikely patrons would be willing to sit through a diatribe about how little customers understand about the chemical process dry-cleaning involves before being allowed to drop off sweaters and shirts. Bye. Off to the dry cleaners down the block.

Human nature being what it is, the need to feel superior is bound to show up in places other than work. However, the one benefit of running into these Nelson clones in other places is that they can be more easily avoided or abandoned. Caught in a conversation with someone who starts discussing minute details of the complex engineering specifications on his latest project at a social gathering? Feel free to simply look across the room, spot a real or imagined acquaintance, and excuse yourself.

Uncomfortably wedged in the crossfire of a "battle of the Bible quotes" between two people who have memorized numerous passages from the Good Book? Even in mid-quote, they can be walked away from with no penalty. Although either one of them could probably Bible-quote everyone else in the room under the table, declining to stand quietly and appear impressed as they slug it out has almost no possibility of retaliation since the likelihood of needing critical information or assistance from them is close to zero. I say "almost" because, although unlikely, there is always the slightest chance that one Bible-quoter or the other could show up at work next week as a new employee.

Interestingly, career academics with extensive backgrounds in literature often seem particularly interested in acting out their own version of Nelson, in their case a game most accurately described as "How Uneducated Can I Make Someone Else Feel?" From a standing start involving discussion on any topic, no matter how unrelated, the career academic will find some way to start dribbling out quotes from all the great classics when holding forth in front of an audience unlikely to have memorized Shakespeare. Sadly, listeners at social events are not the captive audience a class is, and with no grade at stake are free to walk away without raising their hands and asking permission.

For those of us toiling in fields where Nelsons lurk, even when the situation can't be changed, a few precautions are possible to help deal with potential fallout. Of major importance is sending — and keeping copies of — emails outlining the situation and asking for some type of remedy. Optimally, these emails should be sent to at least two people, including Nelson's direct manager. Even knowing that no changes will be made (in fact, Nelson's lame-duck manager didn't even bother responding) those emails can serve as proof of having tried to deal with the situation and been either turned down or ignored. When a "Nelson" suddenly walks out, gets fired, or is gone for other reasons and the finger-pointing starts, it's always good to have documentation. With convincing evidence showing that you brought the situation to the attention of management, who declined to deal with it, the accusatory finger will hopefully move on and find someone else not as well armed.

After emails are sent, and possibly a meeting held to discuss the situation, any further attempts to deal with Nelson from the bottom of the power chain are usually pointless, at best leading to frustration and at worst to job loss. If it comes down to a choice between someone who can cause real disruption by leaving and someone whose tasks can be picked up easily by a coworker, guess who gets walking papers? This is the kind of situation that makes employees think twice about whether or not it's a good idea to be cooperative with other people trying to learn the ropes in their own areas of expertise.

A second tactic is to try having a higher pain threshold than other people affected by a software shithead. If it's possible to put some psychological distance between what's happening and how you react other people with lower tolerance for pain may do the dirty work of trying to get it fixed. Although many situations like this do wind up being addressed after a number of people have quit, those people were faced with the necessity of finding another job while the people who managed to take the abuse and stick it out are still there. If the role of "canary in the coal mine" has to be filled, let someone else volunteer.

However, if it's a situation where you cannot do required work for reasons beyond your control and it's starting to eat up your life, it may be time to simply start looking for another job. The territory between a rock and a hard place has never been a comfortable piece of real estate, and although finding another spot can be difficult, work that chews up stomach lining and sanity for reasons that can't be changed is ultimately not worth having.

The Youth Worshipper

Suddenly, alarms were going off in my head. The mental equivalent of flashing red lights and sirens, an adrenaline spike so strong I could taste it. To make matters worse I was going to have to sit here and appear calm.

It was my first meeting with Kevin, the new department manager. He had been working his way through one-on-one conversations with the roster of employees inherited when a former manager had transferred to another department and Kevin took over. Today was my turn.

First, I sat through a recitation of the usual meaningless platitudes. Work smarter, not harder! Find ways to automate! Think outside the box! Fine so far. Years of keeping a straight face while sitting through this pap gave me the ability to look interested and thoughtful. But then, the conversation turned to what I realized right away was bad news. Smiling, Kevin launched into what I had come to refer to as the "I Love Young People" speech. He "…just loved working with young people. They are so bright, so willing to try new things, to work long hours, so open to new ideas. They would follow instructions instead of arguing. Young people inspired him, he loved sharing new ideas with them..." and so on.

In fact, he continued, it just so happened that he had worked with a wonderful young man in his former department who did the same type of work I was doing. I would love to meet him, my new manager insisted — he could help me out with any problems I might encounter in my work. Gulp. As a more "mature" employee (in the tech industry, this means anyone over thirty-five) I pretty much knew what would happen next. Without knowing how well I was doing my job, Kevin made the assumption that his young former coworker would be better at it.

I'd heard the ILYP sermon many times before, dealt with the bias, and watched as the large companies I'd worked at catered to new college graduates and professional hires in their early twenties in a way that seemed unjustified considering their relatively paltry initial contributions. The company had carefully researched what made new college grads happy and comfortable, then dutifully set up a recreation room for them, complete with pool table, electronic games, and other young-people toys.

They were offered flexible schedules, set up with mentors who made sure their work assignments were appealing and varied, and checked with constantly to monitor their happiness. Great for the new grads and twentysomethings, a bit trying for the rest of us as we reconfigured projects to make sure the interesting and career-building parts were doled out to the young royalty, kept difficult or tedious tasks among ourselves and tried to avoid simmering resentment. We learned to cope with their habit of wearing earphones so they could listen to music. To get their attention you had to get within visual range and signal them to unplug at least one ear long enough to hold a conversation.

Working with these bright young paragons was an interesting experience. With expectations pumped up by graduation from top schools and by recruiters with glowing descriptions of challenging and meaningful work, they would routinely simply decline any task they felt was beneath them. Did the project require working nights or weekends? Sorry, no go — it would cut into free time with friends, which was essential to work-life balance. Meetings at 2:30 in the afternoon? Nope, can't do it. The Butterfly Painting club met then, we would just have to reschedule. Responsibility for maintaining online documentation? Hey, what was the point of getting a top-notch education just to wind up as a glorified file clerk? Find someone else.

Any and all concessions had to be made, as everyone was afraid of being reported to mentors for lack of cooperation during the "onboarding" process. We all wanted to avoid being summoned to meetings with the managers who had been entrusted to usher the promising future of the company through their first years and ordered to explain why we had asked them to do tasks they found distasteful.

One of the highly-touted benefits of a college education is the chance to learn critical thinking. Although some of the new hires seemed to have been at the beach on days when certain technical skills were taught, they had apparently all made it to the critical thinking classes, and found much to criticize in their new jobs. They were full of suggestions on how to improve processes they didn't understand yet, disdainful of careful and detailed testing methodology they didn't know the reason for, and had superior attitudes about coworkers who weren't on Facebook or Twitter. Given the amount of energy the company put into courting them, their attitude was understandable, but that didn't make it any less irritating to put up with.

Every summer, the company managed to have articles written in the local papers extolling the promising futures of this year's wave of grads. They were going to reinvent cloud computing, find ways to map the human genome in ten seconds, and use technology to end world hunger. The applications they wrote would span the globe in a vast array of dazzling colors. Articles about actual accomplishments by older employees languished in obscure peer-reviewed publications and generally merited only a brief mention in internal communications.

To be fair, most of each year's new grads eventually worked out well. Although some left for other jobs as reality set in, most of them eventually outgrew the superior attitude as they ran through their first set of failures, faced up to being dependent on more experienced people to get help, shouldered long-term responsibilities, and started down the decades-long slog of a serious career.

In truth, they were not really the problem. The problem was the prejudicial attitudes exemplified by Kevin's looking at me and assuming, with no knowledge of my competence, that his young and energetic former coworker would be better at my work than I was, would learn new things more quickly, and would have better ideas.

As expected, the inevitable happened. Kevin brought his former coworker over for lunch one day, introduced us, and asked him to "review" my work — just in case there was something there that could be improved. Just a friendly look. Just in case there was an opening in the group, in which case his former right-hand person could be hired and would be able to make a quick start since he would already be familiar with the environment. Just in case...

I'd seen people in this situation react badly and wind up fired, since refusing a direct order from a manager was grounds for dismissal. Knowing what was ahead, I simply verified in an email that Kevin was asking me to turn over passwords and other access to a non-department member, in case there was any question later on about why this was done, and after getting a written response saying to go ahead, handed over passwords. The writing was on the wall so no point in trying to push back.

The group had several other older workers and since we were hearing the "I Love Young People" speech so constantly they also got the message and the transfers started about a month later. Kevin got his wish and used the first vacancy to extend an offer to his former coworker. I was then ordered to hand my work over. It was, Kevin said, time for me to "cross-train in another area" while his shiny new young employee took my place. After years of success and top reviews in my department I was reassigned to menial work. With a good reputation and solid skills, several offers were made as soon as people knew I was looking and I went to work in another department — creating an opportunity for Kevin to hire another of his beloved young people.

When, after years of on-time and trouble-free project completion the department started having trouble meeting deadlines later that year, blame was placed squarely on the employees who had transferred out. They had left an utter mess, Kevin claimed. It was proving difficult to clean up — they hadn't kept up with newer software, documented proce-dures clearly, trained their replacements thoroughly. It was all their fault! There were a host of other excuses: the workload had picked up and become more complex, the department needed more people, other projects were taking more time than estimated to complete. From the safe remove of my new department, this was entertaining to watch.

Why had no one complained to Human Resources? For several very good reasons. First, even when true, discrimi-nation claims are difficult to substantiate, and generally boil down to months, if not years, of wrangling about interpreta-tions of what was said and done. Employees who bring dis-crimination complaints are generally marked as toxic, and can have trouble finding new work.

Second, the next time there is a story in the news about the settlement of a discrimination suit, whether it involves age, race, or anything else, check the dates mentioned in the article. Often the cases have gone on for years, meaning that the people involved lived with a lawsuit hanging over their heads during that time — not a prospect most people would enjoy. Large companies have the resources to wait out and wear down people who bring legal actions against them, no matter how justified those actions are.

The company had lost a few age discrimination suits brought by former employees, but with large, deep corporate pockets, winning a case against the company was rare. Even when department-wide layoffs had seemed like surgical strikes hitting everyone over a certain age, few people had the resources to even try for a legal remedy, generally just accepting whatever severance was offered. Refusing to sign papers waiving the right to sue would have meant no severance package at all.

Interestingly, when the company pension plan was discontinued, things improved slightly for older employees. Since the last five years of service before full pensions kicked in were the most expensive in terms of ramped-up pension commitments, that factor was removed when deciding who to get rid of once the plan was gone. There was still the issue of generally higher pay for older workers, and an army of financial axmen can certainly still be counted on to consider this when making decisions about who stays and who goes.

A few years later when my job was shipped to India I moved on to work for another company, but I still hear the ILYP speech once in a while and have a word of advice to people who inflict this on other employees.

Try looking at it this way: if you were speaking to a black person, would you think it was a good idea to express your thinking this way: "I love white people! White people are so bright, so willing to try new things, to work long hours, and so open to new ideas! White people follow instructions instead of arguing. They inspire me — I love to share ideas with white people..." To a black person on the other side of the conversation, this would not only sound insulting, it might seem like racism, whether it is intended that way or not. If nothing else, a bit of restraint might be called for if only to avoid a potential lawsuit.

Which brings up another aspect of the "I Love Young People" speech. Although the constant flood of warnings to employees urging caution about saying things which could lead to discrimination complaints seems like it would have caused the ILYP speech to be jettisoned, this has turned out not to be the case. The last time I heard it was about a month ago, delivered by a second-level manager during a review, as the first-level manager had just quit. His delivery of the speech was almost word-for-word identical to the one I'd heard from Kevin years ago — and these words are being written at the beginning of 2013.

As they say back east, go figure.

The Verbal Diarrhea Twins

I t was, in theory, a one-hour meeting. The conference room was booked for one hour, and the calendar on my laptop had one hour neatly blocked off. However, the two-hour mark had just come and gone, a mere two agenda items out of five having been disposed of despite numerous attempts to move the discussion along. What had happened?

This meeting was the "perfect storm," a combination of three factors that almost guaranteed that we would run late, reach bad decisions, and stumble out of the room — eventually — numb and dazed.

First, and most critically, this meeting had been graced by the presence of two coworkers whom I had nicknamed "Verbal Diarrhea Guy 1" and "Verbal Diarrhea Guy 2" (nicknames I did not share with other coworkers, for obvious reasons). They were the department's incessant talkers, always ready, willing, and eager to converse spontaneously and at great length on any topic. Either of them was single-handedly capable of extending meeting times by insisting on prolonged discussion of minute details on all issues. And due to some type of complex chemical or psychological interaction I couldn't begin to understand, putting both of them in one room at the same time did not merely double the amount of time they could extend a discussion, but could triple it — or worse.

Second, this was a live meeting. Because all participants were in one building and could be physically present, the meeting organizer had opted not to book a virtual room and reserve a conference phone line. This meant no possibility of merely dialing in, looking at the visuals in a virtual room, and listening through earphones while also flipping through email, or standing up to get the circulation going. The live meeting format required not only our presence, but the pretense of visual attention. Unfortunately, it also gave VDG1 and VDG2 a stage to perform on. As the increasingly far-flung work force meant that live meetings were beginning to dwindle in favor of virtual meetings, the VDG twins were suffering from fewer chances to command the attention of a living, breathing captive audience, and they seemed determined to make the most of every opportunity.

Third, the 3:00 pm start time meant it was unlikely that the conference room we were in was booked after this meeting. As 4:00 had approached, everyone in the room except for the VDG twins was silently praying for the knock on the door, hoping against hope that the room was scheduled for another meeting. It was not to be. At 4:05, as we approached item two on the agenda, VDG1 uttered one of his favorite phrases, words we had all come to dread. "Before we discuss this," he announced, "It's very important that we take a few minutes to go over the background of this issue." With that, he was off and running. Trying to break in would be like trying to get a handhold on a solid wall of glass. His ability to talk for sentences, paragraphs, pages seemingly without drawing breath would be the envy of anchormen and radio announcers everywhere. Could he be sucking in air through hidden gills?

We looked at each other, eyes rolling, nods of sympathy all around, and settled in for a long siege. My head ached. My legs cramped. A revenge fantasy involving some way to obtain a vial of whatever causes laryngitis and getting VDG1 and VDG2 to ingest it sprang into existence in my mind. Any way to do a discreet Google search on causes of laryngitis to take my mind off the incessant droning? Bearing in mind that my company-issued laptop was subject to examination at any time and a search of that type might show up on my browser history, I decided not to chance it.

There followed an hour of listening to the VDG twins bantering back and forth about a detail of earth-shaking importance: should the operational steps we were adding to a published document be labeled a "process" or a "procedure"? Item two was finally dealt with — the decision had been made to refer to the steps as a "procedure." At that point, we would have agreed to anything, no matter how bad or off the mark. With the pain increasing, any further discussion was out of the question. Please, please, please, just let us move on.

My legs were going numb, and my brain was not far behind. The two smokers in the room were getting visibly twitchy. However, experience led us all to try waiting it out due to the consequences of a trip out of the room, which would almost always cause one or the other of the VDG twins to back up the meeting and launch a recap to "fill you in on what you missed while you weren't here." Standing up to stretch our legs would trigger a suggestion that we take a break, which would be followed by the same obligatory recap. We sat. The droning continued. How many inexplicably bad decisions, unworkable product designs, and odd documents are produced in meetings like this, with the run-on talkers holding everyone else hostage?

As we began item three at the two-hour mark, my revenge fantasy sprouted new features. To the vials of laryngitis I would add something that caused a permanent sore throat, one which would be irritated by talking. I could hardly wait to get home to my personal laptop, where browser searches were not available for corporate scrutiny. Forget water-boarding — the military should just hire these two, lock suspects in the room with them, and make it clear that the price of freedom was spilling all those secrets.

Simply announcing that one or more of us had plans that required leaving would have been a zero-sum game. On hearing this, one of the two VDGs could be counted to cheerfully table discussion for now and schedule another meeting. The tradeoff was more pain now against a repeat meeting later on. We looked at each other again, and tacitly agreed to hold on and get it over with.

When the meeting finally ended at 5:30 getting up triggered painful tingling as my legs woke up, and it was a few minutes before the unpleasant sensation wore off. With all five items resolved no further meetings would need to be scheduled for this project, a worthwhile tradeoff for a bit of discomfort. The twins looked a little sad to see us say goodbye and file out of the room.

In some ways, the VDG twins were similar to the motion-sensitive lights that go on, and stay on, whenever there is activity within a certain area. Like those sensors, they would start talking almost as soon as anyone was nearby and run on for as long as a breathing, sentient being was detectable. In one-on-one conversations with either of the twins, most people eventually realized that just making up an excuse — meeting, phone call, need to leave soon — would not work and got up the nerve to walk off, willing to risk the appearance of rudeness to save themselves from a useless and irritating twenty-minute bite out of their day.

As with most of the animals in the office zoo, I am not sure what causes this particular personality tic. Like the tape players who repeat the same stories endlessly, the VDG twins were almost completely impervious to nonverbal cues. When one of them was "visiting" it was pointless to glance at the clock, turn away to work on email, or mention a commitment that required immediate attention. They were like the guests who come to dinner and stay until midnight, ignoring yawns and blithely assuming that when you changed into pajamas it was merely a way to get more comfortable while settling in to enjoy more of their company. The understanding of what causes run-on jabbering I leave to people who know more about psychology than I do. My concern was more pedestrian — coming up with ways to deal with them on a day-to-day basis.

Eventually, I did manage to find two strategies, usable when not in meetings, for getting either of the VDG twins to move on and leave me to work in peace.

The first tactic was one I employed while at my desk, and only worked on these particular chatterboxes because they were both male. I had noticed from long experience that men are uncomfortable when a woman pulls out her purse and starts going through it. Again, I will defer to someone with experience in psychology regarding why this is, but it seems to be universally true. Are they afraid we'll pull out a used tampon or tissue and hand it to them? Start dabbing them with makeup? Brandish a can of spray-on estrogen and douse them with it?

Since there had been an occasional theft of wallets at work, I didn't want to keep my real purse in my cube, and so had gone to Goodwill and bought a large "stunt purse," filling it with an empty "stunt wallet," several tampons, tissues, and an assortment of other filler calculated to insure male uneasiness. In the one exception to having nonverbal cues ignored by the

VDG twins, pulling out my stunt purse, ostentatiously unzipping it, opening it wide, exposing the contents, and plunging a hand into the depths "looking" for something would almost always guarantee a frightened look and a hasty exit. This also worked on other male pests, such as the odd manager or audit compliance worker who came by. However, it had no effect on other women. If, at some later date, I encounter a Verbal Diarrhea Gal, another tactic will have to be thought up.

(In a great example of karmic payback, a few years after originating the "stunt purse" tactic, I got a good taste of what it feels like to be on the receiving end of gender-specific repellent material. During a trip to Atlanta to get training on a storage device, the break room available to students was stocked solely with male-oriented publications dedicated to tattoos, fishing and hunting, motorcycles, cigars and sports — as well as topics of a more, ahem, sexual nature. The most graphic of these publications were quite explicit, showing men and women engaged in diverse and spirited "interactive" activities. The other eleven class participants, all male, could hardly wait for breaks and lunch hour. After the first day, unnerved by sitting in a room full of men thumbing through "Genitalia Quarterly" and "The Babe Spanker's Journal," I decided to use timeouts to take the air by walking around the building, and ate lunch by myself in the lobby.)

The second tactic, which I came to refer to as "forward referral" could be used when away from my cube. For example, occasionally I needed to be in the computer room for several hours until the systems I was setting up were accessible over a network. When one of the VDG twins' sixth sense homed in on a stationary target and brought him over to start chatting, I would manage to appear glad to see him. "Oh," I would say, summoning up a relieved look, "It's a good thing I ran into you. George is starting to work on the XYZ project, and he told me that he was going to look for you to go over the background on the project. He needs lots of very detailed information — and I know you are familiar with XYZ. Can you run by his cube and help him out?" Thinking that a long juicy discussion of details was waiting, off the VDG twin would go. If I was having a particularly quick-thinking day, "George" would be someone who was either away from the office or otherwise unavailable. If not, well, I would apologize and deal with the fallout later on.

The two tactics described above did help when dealing with the twins directly, but various attempts to control the run-on talking in meetings never really worked out. Not for lack of trying, though. We had friends book rooms after one-hour meetings, and got management to try cutting them short. These things only resulted in more meetings being scheduled since we hadn't finished going over agenda items and reaching a consensus.

Although dealing with the immediate issue of taking up other employees' time is one part of dealing with constant talkers, there are others.

One of these is the likelihood of bottlenecks when a run-on talker is responsible for work someone else is waiting for. Being told that someone "Just didn't have time to get to it today" when "it" is something that would have taken ten or twenty minutes is massively annoying when you have seen him standing around talking for hours on end and have a project stalled until he manages to update the access list so you can download documents you need or add notes reporting progress or an issue.

In fairness, the VDG twins did have several good points. One of these was making the "human tape player" seem relatively easy to deal with. The tapes, although repetitive, had fixed and predictable lengths, ending on schedule every time. The twins could go on forever.

Another positive aspect of the VDG twins was their

usefulness as a profit center for contractors being paid on an hourly basis. An hour or two into an extended meeting, there was a dividing line. Those of us who were full-time salaried employees were thinking of how late we'd have to work to make up time, or how early we'd have to get in the next day. The contractors were sitting happily with dollar signs in their eyes, perfectly willing to listen to lengthy speculation about the likely impact of how a product launch was handled on competitor's marketing strategies. When caught in this situation I could only sit back, feign attentiveness, avoid yawning, sneak in useful work if possible while waiting them out, and try not to drown under the waterfall of words.

Those Bastards

The only good thing about this situation was that I didn't have any ice cream in my shopping bag. As the minutes clicked by the annoyance meter ticked toward red, but at least nothing was thawing and dripping. Stopping at the local Safeway to pick up a few things before returning home, I'd run into Ellie. She had recently quit the company we worked for after a long string of issues with management. Now, about five minutes into her "those bastards" recitation, I was clutching my six-pack of paper towels and some kitty litter, gingerly trying to edge away.

However, even though she was an ex-employee now, the bastards apparently still rankled so badly that she just couldn't stop. Although it felt rude to interrupt eventually I broke in, said I had to get going, and took off. Ellie was left with a crestfallen look on her face, unhappy at being deprived of an audience familiar with the cast of characters she was so enthusiastically lambasting.

It was the second time I'd run into her at a local grocery store so she probably lived somewhere near me. If it happened again I would definitely have to look into alternative places to shop.

It's one of the nearly universal facets of the personalities we all bring to work. Almost everyone has some kind of parent or authority issues — or both. The necessary power structure at work means everyone has to deal with the person above them. Even a CEO has a board of directors evaluating performance.

This means that everyone answers to someone who determines work assignments and raises, has to agree to your vacation schedule, decides on your daily work hours, and, in most companies, can monitor what you are doing on your work laptop, read your email, and see what web sites you are visiting. Even in a good situation, one with some maturity on both sides of the relationship, the imbalance of power can be uncomfortable. The most reasonable managers can still wind up dealing with people acting out their unresolved issues with authority figures, serving as a proxy against which those issues are played out.

That Ellie's situations always seemed to be far from good was, we eventually realized, due entirely to her unrealistic expectations and personal problems. Although she had transferred between departments several times, each time expressing her relief to be "out from under the thumb" of whatever hapless first-level manager had been putting up with her, the complaints generally started again within a few weeks of the transfer. We heard it again and again: the new manager was worse than the last one, she didn't know what she was getting into, why hadn't people warned her?

Her continuing unhappiness had seemed particularly odd to the people around her, as the rest of us found the three people she'd worked for easier than average to get along with, and no one else had any complaints. Each manager had listened carefully when she pointed out something that was bothering her, and made adjustments to her workload and environment to accommodate her. However, each concession only seemed to generate more problems.

For example, she had been relocated to a cube nearer to a window because she "needed to be near the light," displacing a disgruntled coworker who was less than happy to be moved inland, but also less likely to complain. Now closer to the window, her new cube was too cold.

Was management trying to give her pneumonia? Facilities workers scrambled to adjust the temperature in her area. At her request, she was allowed to come in an hour later and leave an hour later than other employees   and was upset about traffic being heavier on her way home. Did management realize what a strain it was to be stuck in her car for so much longer? She decided that she should be able to come in later and leave at her original time, working a shorter day, since she often "checked email at night and worked a little on weekends." When that plan was vetoed, she went on a week-long tirade about the abusive, uncaring department head hell-bent on damaging her health. She considered filing a complaint — as she often did — but didn't follow through on it.

To no one's surprise, Ellie had experienced a range of similar issues in previous jobs. In a moment of calm one day at lunch with her, I casually asked if she thought it was possible that her unhappiness with management was self-generated. After all, she had worked for over twenty people in her career — could they all really have been that bad? Could she possibly just be carrying around her attitude with her from job to job? Why was it that the rest of us had no problems with the same managers she had been convinced were picking on her?

No dice. She insisted that her perceptions of all twenty-plus people were correct — they really were that bad. All of them, every single one. She launched a recap of examples "proving" that they'd had it in for her. To the possibility of authority and parent issues causing the problems, I silently added "persecution complex," and sat quietly waiting for the recap to wind down. This was, after all, my own fault for bringing it up.

As bad as Ellie was, at least her constant carping and job changes affected only herself. She was just a temporary irritation to managers, since she relocated so frequently.

In a previous job I'd worked with Rick, a fairly senior technician who made a hobby out of urging people elsewhere in the organization, usually entry-level employees flattered by the attention, to believe that they were being treated unfairly. Rick was determined to convince other employees that those "asshole managers" were a bunch of malicious sadists. He continually urged them to complain, rebel, refuse to cooperate with directions they didn't like, and shirk agreed-to responsibilities.

As a key contributor in the operating system division, Rick got away with playing loud music in his office, sending flaming emails to multiple levels of management, and an array of other offenses which were tolerated because of his skills. Since he generally did get his work done, people in nearby offices were told just to ignore the music or wear ear plugs, and his emails were routinely deleted without any response.

That grudging tolerance, however, was not afforded to those lower down the food chain when, egged on by Rick, they pulled the same stunts. Rick had a knack for finding prey naïve enough not to understand their relatively lower position in the power structure and their much more tenuous hold on their jobs.

Faced with the same insufferable behavior Rick displayed, but coming from workers much more easily replaced, management inevitably decided that it was necessary to make an example of someone. The most logical thing to do was fire the person whose departure would have the least impact.

Having seen this routine several times, it became almost painful to watch. On one occasion, prompted by Rick, a computer operator who worked the very desirable day shift during the week decided to simply refuse when asked to change his schedule slightly to align with an alteration in the three shifts which provided twenty-four hour coverage for the IT infrastructure. Convinced by Rick that his seniority entitled him to demand that management allow him to continue with the old schedule, Dave coolly informed his manager that the change was simply unacceptable. Even after being issued a formal first warning, Dave continued to refuse, as Rick assured him that management must surely be bluffing.

When Dave was fired, he was stunned. Hadn't Rick said that management would back down? From his safe berth in the upper reaches of the operating system department Rick offered a cursory apology. Oops, sorry. Guess they were serious. As one of a number of employees who had approximately the same skills, Dave was expendable in a way that Rick wasn't. For Rick, this had been entertainment. For Dave, it was a life-changing event, leaving him feeling used and bitter. There are definitely less painful ways to have your eyes opened about how and why someone might want to influence your behavior and choices.

After sharing the termination news with his understandably furious wife and reviewing his personal finances that night, Dave marshaled a humiliating apology in a phone call to his manager the next day, and asked for his job back. No way. Fed up with having to deal with people Rick had influenced, management felt that making an example of Dave would help to keep everyone else in line.

For a while, it did. However, with the constant turnover of employees in the operations department supplying a steady stream of naïfs who hadn't seen this happen before,

Rick usually managed to find another mark. Employees who had been at the company long enough to see several cycles of the pattern play out would often try to warn people Rick was suddenly being friendly with, but usually to no avail.

For the rest of us, trying to get through our days with as little excitement as possible meant keeping what Rick did and said in perspective, being alert to his hidden agenda, and not taking his opinions seriously. On the heels of any assignment change or workload increase Rick could always be counted on to come by and remark on how unreasonable the request was and what a strain it would be, trying his best to gin up ill will. Familiar with Rick's issues, the best way to deal with him was simply to agree, but ignore everything he said. No point arguing with Rick to his face, which would only generate an accusation about being co-opted by "the enemy," but also no point in screwing up our own lives for his amusement.

For management, dealing with this was not simple. By signaling their willingness to tolerate Rick's obnoxious behavior but enforce the letter of the law with more expendable employees, they laid the company open to complaints of unequal treatment, and after the occasional firing were asked to explain why rules were enforced unevenly. Since Rick's antics went undocumented while the operators were formally warned the first time they pushed back, the fig leaf of no written complaints against Rick seemed to satisfy human resources, but left no doubt in anyone's mind that the actual difference in treatment was due to how much more easily replaced lower-level employees were.

Since management declined to deal with the root cause of the issue the pattern continued, with the occasional sacrifice of an employee gullible enough to put his job on the line and become collateral damage in Rick's vendetta against authority.

The Expatriate Community

The question only hung in the air for about a week. Tim had given notice on a Friday, and been instantly walked out of the building. The immediate escorted exit for anyone giving notice who is going to work for a competitor is standard practice in the tech industry. This ritual is a little silly since if someone wanted to steal secrets, copy files, wreak any other type of havoc, or recruit coworkers to come along to the new company it's already been done by then. In the few minutes between the time Tim let us know he was leaving and his march out the door we did the standard exchange of non-work user accounts so we could keep in touch and made the usual jokes about finding spots for us at the new place. Then we watched him walk out of the building with a cardboard box full of desk toys, pictures of his family, and service awards, flanked by his manager and someone from company security.

To no one's surprise a week later the question — was this an isolated event or the first in a continuing string of resignations? — was answered. Someone who had worked for Tim gave notice, then two people from another group who had worked with Tim and I on projects. All were going to the same startup and would form the nucleus of a new group — managed by Tim. All got the same somewhat envious goodbyes, cardboard box, and escort to the parking lot. The next week one more person, who had worked for Tim before transferring to another group, joined them.

A few days after the last resignation we had lunch at a local restaurant with the people who had quit and got more details. There were, in fact, jobs still open. Were any of us interested? The new company was growing fast, and had a great product. The inducements they listed were standard startup bait: the company might go public, people joining now would get stock, it was going to be an adventure. Their enthusiasm was catching, and left the rest of us wondering if joining them might be a good idea.

Common in almost all industries, the formation of these "expatriate" communities, groups of people moving from one company to another either all at once or over a few weeks or months, has some interesting aspects, not just for the people relocating but for those of us left behind and for the companies on both sides of the move.

For my excited former coworkers, there were some great initial benefits. One of the things that make these expat groups work well is that they select each other. People will seldom recruit coworkers they dislike to join them at new companies so the very fact that they bring in people they like gives the group a better than even shot at harmony. They know each others' work styles, strengths, and weaknesses. The four who left after Tim had worked together on several successful projects. Each of them got a good bump in salary to relocate. The person who brought in the résumés for the expats wound up getting recruitment bonuses for each of them — expensive for the company, but very profitable for the guy turning in the résumés.

Another benefit of relocating, whether as part of an expat community or not, is the temporary "weightlessness" of being between jobs. The most carefree time for employees can be the few weeks between giving notice (or in Tim's case knowing you are leaving but haven't given official notice yet) and the time you actually change jobs. As a "lame duck" employee, do you really care whether things get done or not? No worries about the future of your projects — you won't be here to deal with whatever is going to happen. Long work days? Forget it — at 5:00 pm you can just stroll out, since it no longer matters what anyone thinks. Long, boring meeting? No problem. Just call in with a "flat tire." Sorry, I'll be in as soon as the tow truck gets here — you can fill me in about what happened at the meeting later on.

Although the change of scenery and the excitement of joining an expat group can be appealing, there are some definite risks. A few weeks after a group of coders left at a previous company, we started getting calls asking if their old jobs had been filled yet. As often happens, there was a bit of a disconnect between the glowing descriptions of what their new jobs would offer and reality.

Eventually a few of them were rehired and brought back some interesting stories. Apparently the wide-open horizons and chance to work on cutting-edge technology promised during recruitment had turned into twelve-hour days of mind-numbing and repetitive tasks which had been deserted when the last group of coders got fed up and left. The latest group of expats had been caught up in the tech startup business model generally described as: "Bring them in, burn them out, lay them off or wait until they quit, bring in new ones, repeat." Although a new job can be a step up the ladder financially and in terms of work assignments, it can just as easily be a ticket to the last act of "March of the Lemmings."

One of the most common signs of this type of "buyer's

remorse" is the appearance on LinkedIn or other job-related sites of expat résumés soon after a job change. Since the most active users are those who are either recruiting or looking for work, when someone who has just moved to a new company starts popping up active a few weeks later, this could mean a serious rethinking about the new job. If more than one or two people signal that they're looking to return to the company of origin or move to yet another company the migration may have been a bad idea from the start. This was difficult for the would-be returnees, but reassuring to the rest of us who had chosen to stay put.

Even if the recruiting hype and reality are a closer fit, another risk is the tendency of mass hiring to be followed by mass layoffs. Companies which grow quickly are likely to be unstable, both in terms of integrating new employees and developing business. Startups and small companies are likely to be dependent on a limited number of contracts, projects, or new venture capital funding. If something happens to one large contract or the next round of funding dries up, layoffs are much more likely than at companies with more sources of income, a bigger financial cushion, and a number of other lines of business to absorb employees who were involved in cancelled contracts.

Another risk of joining an expatriate tribe is the inevitable jockeying for position on projects and in departments. In a new and different environment, even a group that got on well before emigrating has to sort out roles and workloads. Since everyone is new at about the same time, in the free-for-all atmosphere where workloads are configured, someone has to wind up on the short end.

For employees left behind there are also some good and some bad aspects of saying goodbye to so many people at once. On the up side, any interesting or career-building work abandoned by the departures is up for grabs.

One of the most interesting projects I've ever worked on was acquired as a result of mass resignations. The abrupt departure of both the person responsible for that work and his manager left the project, along with several others, orphaned. Realizing that no one was sure who would be running things, I decided to try grabbing it without consulting anyone.

Calculating that the straightforward approach had the best chance of success, I simply sent out an email to the remaining participants announcing that I was the new project leader, and letting everyone know that the weekly meetings would continue. Priorities for the project, as well as individual assignments would now be set by me but, as the email generously pointed out, I would be glad to consider their input.

Interestingly, no one ever asked about this, although I had a credible cover story prepared in which the departing manager had asked me to take over before he quit. This was a fairly safe untruth since before leaving he had generated so much hostility that no one was communicating with him. Except, at least fictitiously, me.

As it turned out, I got away with this for a very simple reason. People in the upper level of management assumed that the group had discussed this among ourselves and decided that I should head the project. The other people in the project assumed that I had discussed it with management and been asked to be take the lead. Fortunately for me, these groups did not communicate with each other. It was also a challenge for me not to ask people if they noticed what I had done, since it seemed like such a peculiar approach to have worked.

The opportunistic "grab first" approach also had another benefit. When it came time for the more boring or trivial projects left behind by the departures to be reassigned, I could point out that having already picked up part of the workload I should not be expected to take on anything else.

On the downside, those of us left behind were dealing not

only with an increased workload but gaps in specific types of expertise. Like most groups, whether tech-related or not, some people are stronger than others in certain areas, and all work of that type gravitates toward them. One of the people who left had the strongest skills in the group in setting up complicated network switches and troubleshooting network connectivity problems. Another had been expert in working the frustrating and obscure hardware procurement system, a torturous process that had managers all over the company tearing their hair out.

Like many companies, although lip service was given to the concept of cross-training, the reality was that the limited size of the staff and the constant pressure of schedules meant that almost all of us had skills that were unique in the group. For a few months we thrashed around and lost a lot of time to network problems, but eventually we grew the expertise we needed and things smoothed out.

For the companies on both ends of a mass migration there are a range of issues to be dealt with. At the acquiring company, bringing in an established pre-fab group can help get the projects they were hired to work on running quickly. However, I've seldom seen an entire group come in and not engender at least some resentment from current employees. The newcomers can be insular, protective of their territory, and hostile to "outsiders." Having become something of a clan, people outside their group will have the role of "other," and will be treated accordingly. Often the territory handed to an expat group was something existing staff members were interested in, and being frozen out by people who have just arrived is bound to create bad feelings.

There is also the question of copyright and intellectual property issues. Since the "capital" of most tech companies are ideas as well as code, the migration of key staffers who generated those ideas and worked on that code to a competitor can be crippling. Although some employees are required to sign agreements not to work for competitors within a certain length of time after termination, most are not.

There are always a handful of lawsuits in progress regarding poached employees with critical skills and knowledge — and probably will be forever. For companies on the losing end of an expatriate migration, this has to be frustrating, as a mass migration leaves them not only to shuffle the remaining staff or start hiring, but also to think about whether or not to fire up the lawyers and crank out more lawsuits.

Attempts to stop people from leaving are usually pointless, though. The modern-day work-for-money model most of us are engaged in is employment, not slavery or indentured servitude. The company is free to fire us — and we are free to go.

Having been part of an expatriate community several times I know firsthand what an easy transition it can be, and also how badly it can work out.

My first experience with a mass migration was a move from a company that was in a very obvious death spiral, and the crew was abandoning ship as quickly as new jobs could be found. When a manager who had bailed out a few weeks previously called and asked me to interview at his new company, I jumped at the chance and wound up being offered a job. The group he was managing consisted of fourteen people — twelve of whom were the grateful recipients of life jackets tossed to us as our old company foundered. He had managed most of us before and selected a team that worked together almost perfectly until the time, about five years later, that most of our jobs were shipped to another country.

The second time, things did not work out as well. Relocating with several colleagues to a new company, we soon realized they had hired more of us than were really needed. The company had optimistically assumed a growth pattern involving new contracts which did not materialize, leading to the necessity of laying off two of the six people who had come in together.

Although the manager who had convinced each of us to give up stable jobs for the new company was regretful and apologetic, there was no way around it — two of us had to go. Fortunately for me, I was not one of the two, but nothing could have brought home more clearly the risks involved in leaving a solid company for what had been described as a more "dynamic" environment. All of us knew the risks when we made the decision to relocate, and had been fully aware of the possible consequences.

It probably would have been a better idea to look a little harder and wait a little longer before I leapt but this time, at least, luck was on my side.

Termination

. . . .

There was an elephant sitting with us in the cafeteria, huge, distracting and so difficult to talk about that after a few perfunctory words we avoided it entirely. Polite chit-chat has its time and place, and we stuck to topics similar to what the English refer to as "the roads and the weather," impersonal and meaningless.

The same group of coworkers sitting at this lunch table carefully parsing their words had all been here a week ago ripping unselfconsciously through a spirited discussion about what was up with the latest project, news, family vacation. What was the elephant, and how did it get here?

In the last week, one of the people at this table, Sammy, had been through the firing/rehiring procedure known as "outsourcing in place." Last week he'd had about the same salary we all had, the same benefits, the same amount of time with the company.

However, last Wednesday he had been approached by his manager and informed that his position, along with twenty-four others, was being "reclassified." It would no longer be performed by someone employed directly by the company, instead being filled by a contractor who worked for an agency. Would Sammy be interested in applying to that agency for his job? If so, he would almost certainly be hired — after all, he already knew the job pretty well. If not, he would be terminated. Hit with the sudden simultaneous layoff and offer of rehire Sammy, like almost everyone else facing the same situation, grabbed the offer and was given the contact information for the contracting company that would be filling his job.

Sammy was back at work on Monday. Same cube, same job. However, his salary was now about twenty percent less than it had been a week ago, with a portion of that going to the outsourcing company. His job now carried no health benefits, no retirement program, no 401K match, an annual amount of paid vacation roughly a third of what he'd had as a direct employee, and even less job security — if that was possible. He could be let go with a phone call to the contracting agency, which would simply call Sammy and tell him not to return to work the next day. His wife was calling around today, comparison shopping for health insurance, dealing with the shock of how much more expensive it is to purchase privately than through an employer.

We were sympathetic to Sammy and his family for what they were going through. However, we were all quietly relieved that it hadn't happened to us, and were thinking the same thing: am I next? Could it happen to me? How would I deal with it? We were mentally cycling through predictable responses that are similar to the stages of grief, from bargaining to denial to resignation to thoughts on how to prepare in case the next round of outsourcing hit home. Would there be any point in working harder, putting in more hours, taking on more responsibility? How long would savings last if income was reduced or eliminated entirely? Was there enough other income in the household to cover expenses in case of a layoff?

Meanwhile the company was going through its own calculus on the other side of the issue: which jobs could be outsourced in place, offshored, or eliminated entirely without impacting business? How much money could be saved if more workers were reduced to part-time?

Like a lot of ways in which the workscape has changed in the last twenty years, the era of increasingly common employment practices similar to "outsourcing in place" had been bookended by a long-ago-and-far-away time when what happened to Sammy would have been unthinkable. In the once-upon-a-time that seems like a fairy tale now, we couldn't have imagined how routine, even expected, sudden terminations and the variety of other encroachments on our ability to make a living would become.

In fact, the type of outsourcing Sammy had just undergone was one of the easier ones to deal with. He was still employed, had most of his former salary, and a week of vacation. These things gave him a chance to look for another job while still working, a great advantage since many companies prefer to hire from among people who are currently employed. This is unfortunate since so many of the unemployed or underemployed wind up that way through no fault of their own. Although it's true that skills need to be updated continuously, a few months without a job shouldn't take otherwise good workers out of consideration for openings.

Since he still had a job, Sammy had a little breathing room to think about whether to stay or look around for another position. Each of the variety of modern-day transitions from full-time work to either total unemployment, reduction in hours, or cuts in pay have different "Sword of Damocles" aspects.

There it is, over your head, bound to fall some time, but when, and how? The corrosive effects of uncertainty are well-known, but following what had happened to Sammy it was hard to avoid worrying. Before the lunch table had lapsed into meaningless chat Sammy, always a bit of an optimist, had pointed out a few ways in which his situation could have been much worse. One by one I thought through the possibilities he had mentioned and tried to think about how I would cope with each one.

The sudden appearance of a manager carrying a cardboard box would have signaled the beginning of sudden complete unemployment. Depending on the shape the company was in, there might be some severance pay — but if not, unemployment insurance might be the only assistance available as the search for a new job began. A quick check of my bank accounts told me I was unprepared for this. Any way to save more money? Maybe it was time to improve my notoriously scattered shopping habits, best described as: a) see something I like; b) buy it.

The workplace version of "musical chairs" was also becoming popular. Employees are given notice that their jobs will either be eliminated entirely or offshored and are given a month or so to find other jobs inside the company. Unfortunately, there are usually a much higher number of people looking to relocate than there are "chairs" for them to land in, and when the music stops, some are bound to be left standing — or, in this case, walking out the door. When it looks like the music is about to end, it's time to start cozying up to managers in other departments who might be deciding who gets to fill the available "chairs." Maybe a little "volunteer" work on projects visible to those managers was in order.

Another possibility was the long, slow, dreadful dead-employee-walking phenomenon in which people were required to train their own replacements overseas before being terminated. One of the most difficult of transitions to cope with, being told to turn your job over to someone else always carried the threat of instant firing for refusing to cooperate. Being let go for this reason was a double whammy: not only no severance package, but no unemployment insurance, since it was not available to people who had been fired for cause.

Some years ago, I was on a team of hardware testers when we were informed that our jobs were being sent to China just as soon as we trained our Chinese replacements. Finding innovative ways to stall the transition while we scouted other openings inside and outside the company sparked some very interesting creative streaks.

The following year became a battle of wills. We, of course, wanted to keep our jobs for as long as we could, while management's fondest desire was to drop-kick our butts off the payroll as quickly as possible. Using the time and language differences as props for our efforts, most of us relocated within the company and only one person actually wound up being laid off.

The gradual financial starvation of reduced hours can also be hard to deal with. As employers find more creative and automated ways to schedule workers, keeping each employee below the number of hours per week that would trigger required benefits becomes easier. This used to be most common in industries like retail sales and service, but with increasingly sophisticated project-tracking software available, is also appearing in high-tech, allowing companies to keep their obligation to provide benefits and paid vacations to a minimum.

My plan for this eventuality was to accept part-time status and start looking for another full-time job or a second part-time job if necessary. I already knew several people who were working multiple jobs, each one below the amount of hours that would have earned benefits, and although it had the feeling of a cobbled-together living, they were at least making ends meet.

While I was on one half of the seesaw thinking about coping with winding up on the downside, the company was contemplating how to improve their own financial position and wind up on top. In addition to all of the methods listed above, another great way to save money is to replace workers with H1B visa holders. Even though outsourcing to other countries has picked up steam in the last twenty years, some companies still prefer employees who are present on site. To save money on labor when the employee-in-chair-on-premises employment model is preferred, some companies simply laid off most of the people in certain departments then replaced them with guest workers.

Although the H1B program is supposed to impose conditions requiring a search for qualified citizens before offering jobs to guest workers, the same bright legal minds finding ways to reclassify employees into categories for which no benefits are owed by the company have turned their attention to this issue. It is now common to find entire departments populated with nothing but H1B visa holders making substantially less than the workers they replaced.

On a certain level, all of these things were easy to understand. Just like companies, individuals will do things that are in their own best financial interests. If the person mowing my lawn is being paid $100 a month, and someone else was willing to do the same work for $80, I would go with the lower-priced gardener unless there was some overriding reason to make an economic decision based on non-economic factors.

All of these things were in the thought balloons wafting over the heads of the lunch table crowd as we watched twenty-five of our coworkers transformed into contract employees. Our company was far from the only one going through this transition. Since we were competing with others vendors who sold the same products, if our prices weren't competitive the impact might be much worse than outsourcing part of the workforce.

We'd seen other companies that were slow to adjust to new employment models fail as more nimble competitors were able to drop prices once labor costs had been reduced. The reasons for outsourcing are clear and perfectly valid — just a little hard to live with, at least for most of the people at the lunch table. We were all pretty far along in our careers and had been working during the decades when the transition from relatively secure employment to the "Sword of Damocles" era took place.

In that former once-upon-a-time when most of us had started working there was a general expectation that if you were doing excellent work, got along with everyone, and were lucky enough to work for a company that was healthy and profitable, prospects for keeping your job were good. Today, it may not matter how healthy the company is, how well you get along, or how excellent your work is. It isn't being the best, it's being the cheapest that is often the deciding factor in keeping your job, and in this category workers in different states or countries often win out. For us, coming to terms with this had been a big adjustment.

But for the generation of workers just starting out it may be that perennial job insecurity won't bother them as much as it bothers us. The nature of employment has become so ephemeral that people launching careers now know they should plan for a number of terminations, and so may be more comfortable being laid off occasionally regardless of their commitment to their jobs or the quality of their work.

At this point, a disclaimer is in order: employed for over thirty years in high-tech, I've never been laid off. There have, however, been many occasions when I moved to a new job ahead of a probable layoff, transferred to get away from a bad situation, been offered something better, or decided to jump ship if a company was looking iffy. Since loyalty to a company, much like loyalty to employees, has become a quaint relic of the past, I have changed jobs several times when doing so created problems for an employer, and done so with a clear conscience.

For example, at one point I became part of a "revenge hiring" specifically engineered to have a negative impact on my employer. A manager, who had been fired from the small company we both worked at after a number of arguments with occupants of the executive suite, knew of a job at another company that would be a step up for me. He arranged to have the hiring manager, a friend of his, call and ask me to come in for interviews. My eventual departure caused serious problems that resulted in IT being outsourced. However, the new position carried such a significant salary increase that when I told a relative about it, without hearing another detail about the job she had simply gasped and said "Take the job! Just call them up tomorrow and tell them you'll take it!" I did, and never looked back. The company I was leaving wasn't doing too well, and there was no point in waiting around for the cardboard box.

Even with a lot of caution and constant carefulness, I have to admit that there has been at least some luck involved in managing to string together thirty years without facing unemployment. As my brother, familiar with the dynamics of employment in high-tech, puts it, my career has been like running through a rainstorm without getting hit by a single drop.

Journey to the Dark Side

··

Donald's journey to the dark side had begun, and the rest of us waited anxiously to see what would happen. Until he returned, the thick, paralyzing miasma of dread would hang over us.

After two years as a coworker Donald had decided to apply for the management job left vacant when our previous manager retired. Having seen a number of times what happened when a former peer was promoted over his own group, we had good reason to worry. Donald was away for the week at new-manager orientation classes. We waited, distracted and concerned.

Would he, like previously promoted coworkers, resemble the pod people in "Invasion of The Body Snatchers" when we saw him again — physically identical to the original Donald but reborn soulless and mindless as a result of his transformative experience?

The running joke about the three operations performed on newly-minted managers — castration, heart removal, and lobotomy — ran through our minds, but somehow didn't seem quite so funny this week. As someone in another group had pointed out after struggling to explain a project delay due to snags his former-technician-now-manager used to experience but now refused to believe could have an impact, "It's like something happens and they turn stupid."

All of us in the group were also running through two years' worth of memories about what we had shared with Donald. He was familiar with our uncensored opinions about management and had even joined in some of those discussions, venting about the latest unrealistic schedule, strange request, or unnecessary meeting. But what else? Personal information that seems harmless to share with a colleague was often not a good idea to share with management. Would decisions about assignments, transfers and layoffs be affected by what he knew?

One group member had confided that he was starting a business outside work, and if things went well, would be in a position to quit. Would he be Donald's first choice to lay off if someone had to go? Be watched closely to see if he was working on his business during the day? I had shared my critical opinions about some of the people who were now Donald's peer managers. Would he share this information with them since they were now his tribe? Worse, a member of our group had entertained us one recent evening over beers with descriptions of his attempts to get someone on another team to go out with him, even after being rejected the first few times. Could that now be construed as harassment? Would he be dispatched to sensitivity training or given the dreaded "warning"?

Another uncomfortable aspect of Donald's new promotion was that he would now know all of our salaries, information we generally did not share with coworkers. He would also be deciding on raises and other details of our day-to-day assignments. As the week wore on, the tension rose.

Next Monday, Donald was back. He was now more

reserved and careful about what he said, which was certainly to be expected from someone who had just gone through a week of classes on how to avoid saying or doing anything that could trigger complaints, lawsuits, or accusations of unequal treatment. We were uncomfortable around him, but at least he had moved to an office on the perimeter of the cube farm and so would not be watching us on a minute-to-minute basis. This was a situation where a little bit of distance is a good thing.

At our first group meeting after his return, it wasn't immediately apparent whether or not the pod people had won. We sat through a discussion of how beneficial his technical background and hands-on work would be in making him a good manager. He understood, he said, the problems in predicting how long it would take to solve a problem that had never been encountered before, of doing creative work on a schedule, of dealing with projects that really needed some concentration to make progress on when each day brought a number of attention-fracturing interruptions. It sounded too good to be true and sure enough, it was.

Gradually, it became apparent that the three operations and journey through the management-training pod farm had worked the predictable effect on Donald. A mere six weeks later, sitting in his new office, I found myself in the middle of a protracted discussion on why the chart showing progress on one of my current projects displayed a forty-five percent completion status, when it should have been sixty-five percent by now. Had he read the stream of emails sent in the last few weeks describing how a field emergency had caused two of the project participants to be away unexpectedly? How a projected software configuration turned out to be unworkable, necessitating a redesign which in turn required backtracking and redoing some of the setup?

Well, yes, he had read them. But he also knew that I

always padded schedules by a few weeks to allow for emergencies. So, all things considered, the project really should be at sixty-five percent. Regretting my former openness in discussing this with him, I was angry with myself for sharing so much. Having seen peers get promoted before I should have known better, but Donald had never expressed an interest in moving up, so my guard had been down.

Unlike many fields, high-tech offers relatively good salaries even at the bottom of the ladder. With a few years of experience, programmers, network engineers, and administrators can make a good living wage, even in a high-cost-of-living area like Silicon Valley. In many other fields this is not true, which makes the move into management in those fields understandable. But in an industry where technicians often have higher salaries than their first-level managers, it can be hard to understand what prompts people to apply for management jobs. My own reasons for turning down chances to go into management involved concerns about budgets, personnel issues, reviews, and paperwork. Veteran managers found my list amusing and seriously incomplete, pointing out that if those were the only problems, hey, it would be a cakewalk.

After finishing up the review of my projects I worked up the nerve to ask Donald why he had decided to move up. His answers were among those I'd heard from other new managers after the promotion and before reality set in. They knew they could do a better job than almost any other manager they had worked with. If they didn't accept the promotion the other person being considered would cause mass resignations that would wreck their group. They were exhausted by the daily grind of hands-on technical work, disliked working nights and weekends, and had trouble keeping up with the constant need to retrain and pick up new skills. The roller-coaster ride of extreme highs and lows took a toll on personal life. Stress contained behind a gritted-teeth calm facade at work showed up at home and the yelled-at spouse and kids or kicked dog had just about had it.

Given all of the above, a move up to the first rung of process-jockey territory, where expectations seemed to center largely around making sure compliance work and other required administrative tasks got done on schedule, personnel issues were quashed before becoming a problem for the company, projects were efficiently shepherded, and layoffs were handled when necessary seemed like a good move. How hard could it be?

Well, as it turns out, harder than it looks. After talking to a number of people I'd known first as technicians and later on as managers in different tiers of the org chart, a much more complete picture of the difficulties emerged.

Apparently, management is one of those things like parenthood: people who think they can do a much better job than those frazzled parents chasing their out-of-control kids around the park invariably don't have any first-hand experience. And just like new parents who suddenly find that constant exhaustion and an endlessly crying baby affect their master plan to be paragons of patience and control, when the uncomfortable realities of day-to-day management set in perspectives can change.

One of the first challenges for promoted technicians is having to let go of involvement in project details. When work on the next release of Donald's former project started, his attendance at technical background meetings became awkward as he offered suggestions for approaches that were no longer relevant. Uncomfortable with the politely blank silences and refusal to make eye contact following his suggestions, he eventually took the hint and stopped attending reviews. Letting go of the skills that previously were what earned a living has to be like letting go of a lifeline.

Next up was the difficulty of actually being expected to

deal with personnel issues, a much different experience than merely whining or laughing about them with coworkers, and hunting for creative and undetectable ways to circumvent or neutralize the problems.

In addition to listening to his new subordinates complaining about the office monitor, the verbal diarrhea twins, Nelson's latest refusal to cooperate, or the endlessly shirking work "passenger" whose tasks were being offloaded to resentful coworkers, he was now actually expected to do something about these situations. However, as he pointed out, unless something was carefully documented and "actionable" according to company policy there wasn't really anything he could do. Even though the logic of this position was understandable, it didn't stop the resentment about his lack of action.

While there wasn't much Donald could do about some of the low-level annoyances, there were other areas where he was required to act: enforcing policies made by higher-ups whether he agreed with them or not. Although most of the people in our group were experienced enough in how large corporations worked to understand that Donald was just the messenger and may not have agreed with the latest bad strategic decision or peculiar austerity measure, to us he was the face of those decisions and had to deal with the blowback. Gradually he learned, as most managers did, to appear to be listening to our concerns, to make the appropriately sympathetic comments, and then do nothing.

Another issue which seems to startle new managers the first few times it happens is being blind-sided by things which everyone else knew about way in advance. When our coworker with the business was finally doing well enough to quit, everyone in the group knew about it a month out. Unsure whether or not he would get the cardboard-box-and-escort treatment, he waited until a few days before his planned exit to give notice, taking Donald completely by surprise and leaving a hole in the middle of several projects.

Other last-to-know issues that Donald had to deal with during his tenure as captain of a ship he used to crew on involved projects that were failing, designs that were unworkable, and one person with a health issue that eventually required an extended leave of absence. Perhaps it was an underlying expression of displeasure or even resentment about his promotion but in each of these situations Donald was the last to know, finding out about the issues only after serious hits to completion schedules, and receiving notice of the planned medical leave two days before it started. He was angry at the lack of advance notice, but with the amnesia resulting from the requisite lobotomy had forgotten that when he was an oar-puller, he was just as unlikely to give the former manager a heads-up when bad news was brewing.

Also increasingly frustrating for Donald was the need to rely on other people to complete work that would affect his own reviews and chances to move further up. At the bottom of the pile, you can always put in a few more hours or dispatch emails explaining why something isn't getting done, and are mainly responsible for work in your own area of expertise. If your coworkers screw up their own projects, it isn't your problem.

Now that he was overseeing people whose technical specialties he had no background in, Donald couldn't be sure if making progress was really as difficult as people sending the my-project-is-stalled emails made it sound, or whether they were just goofing off. Could he really trust what we were saying? Should he use the standard threat of hiring a contractor to "help" if work didn't speed up?

After about eight months the inevitable happened and Donald had to lay off one of his former coworkers. Even though one person had left under his own power and the

opening hadn't been filled, the cuts required that one addi-
tional person be let go from our group. The unfortunate thing
about across-the-board cuts is that they hit departments that
are already being efficiently run or are understaffed dispro-
portionately hard. The decision Donald made must have been
particularly painful, as the person let go needed employment
to keep his green card. Given the mix of skills in the department, the decision was probably a good one but for days after
it was over, Donald was even more quiet and withdrawn than
he had been in the months since his promotion.

Was he regretting the move? After making serious decisions most people will wind up playing the "was it a good
decision or a bad decision?" tape in their minds for a while. If
the answer is "good decision," the tape stops after a relatively
short time. However if the answer is "bad decision," the tape
will be playing for a lot longer, if not forever. Being able to let
go and move on when the tape replay keeps stopping on "bad
decision" is very difficult.

After about sixteen months of limping through encoun-
ters with the new reality of life in charge, Donald quit and
moved on to do project-oriented work at a smaller company
where he would no longer be managing people. Even after all
that time, his exit was a relief for him and for us.

Although Donald decided on a strategic retreat, many
other new managers seem to make the adjustment, deal with
the problems, and continue up the food chain or off to other
departments when things heat up. These managers seem to
accept the problems that being in charge involves, and develop
their own coping strategies.

In my years of toiling in high-tech I've probably worked
for about twenty-five people. Exactly two of those have been
great managers, getting incredible performance out of their
teams, respect from the people both above and below them
in the organization and a long line of applicants any time a

slot opened up in their groups. Donald was not one of them.

The other twenty-three have ranged from passable to find-another-job-as-soon-as-possible. But every time I see a "Donald" venture into management, my respect for those two increases, as does my conviction that turning down my own chances to move up definitely landed on the "good decision" side of the tape.

The Tower of Babel

This, I thought glumly, must be what it's like to be a dog. A serious discussion was going on around me, but I was unable to understand anything except one or two technical terms that apparently didn't translate into Urdu. Every now and then a recognizable word floated by and my ears would perk up in the same way that a dog might suddenly be attentive when the words "walk" or "leash" are mentioned. Like Fido, I was trying to figure out what was going on. However, unlike Fido, I wasn't content to sit patiently wagging my tail, happy just to be hanging out while waiting to see if a nice walk was in the offing. I wanted more information.

The subject being addressed was apparently a problem with one of the several network programs my work group tested. The acronyms for these programs kept popping up in the middle of otherwise unintelligible — at least to me — sentences, so I pretty much knew what was going on. Unfortunately, there was no way for me to tell if a solution was being proposed, some new roadblock had turned up, or results from the latest failed test run were being analyzed.

We all had ideas about what was wrong and how to

proceed, but with a limited amount of equipment and a short time frame to get past the latest snag, we needed to reach a consensus and start trying fixes. After everyone had apparently had their say and some kind of agreement was reached, one of the discussion participants went over to his laptop, logged into the test complex, made several changes, and restarted the test. I asked about the change being tested but was brushed off: never mind, it was a long story, this is what they had decided to do. I was free to observe test results when they were posted — someone would fill me in later.

In addition to the problem of being excluded from the general discussion which had just taken place, there was a second issue. After working with the failed test the day before, I had done some research, tried a few things, and logged some results. One of those looked promising, but there was no way to tell if my coworkers had considered the logs from those tests during their discussion. Were they about to waste time covering ground I'd already been over?

As well as possibly having something to gain if I could have been included in the conversation, I may have had something to contribute which would not only avoid duplication of effort, but perhaps spark some new ideas about the root cause of the problem or ways to move forward. It's hard to be a good team player when everyone else is sending and receiving signals in a language I can't understand.

The last twenty years have seen an influx of workers from a multitude of countries into Silicon Valley and elsewhere. As the workforce has diversified, "language vectors" consisting of people with common ethnic and linguistic backgrounds have evolved. It is perfectly understandable that people are more comfortable communicating in their native language than one into which thoughts and words have to be translated.

Employees who share a common language frequently find ways to work on the same project, making communication easier. If everyone in a work group speaks Tagalog, there is no need to speak English at meetings. Like the cliques in high school, these language vectors also seem to segregate in the cafeteria, where specific ethnic groups always seem to have certain tables staked out.

Although these things are logical and make the workplace more comfortable for non-English speakers, they do make English-only speakers like me the odd man out. The languages being spoken in my cubehood are probably common everywhere by now: Chinese, Vietnamese, Urdu, Spanish, Malay. The group would have had an even broader diversity quotient, but the Sri Lankan and the Iranian had left for another company a while ago. And the foreign languages spoken by the cube dwellers around me are only part of the overall picture. In conference calls to Bangalore, Israel, and Brussels, although English is the spoken language accents are often so thick that I can't pick up much more about what is being said than when the discussion is in Vietnamese. Interestingly, the accents of the Belfast team leave me almost as lost at sea as those from Bangalore.

As obvious a solution as it seems there were several reasons why it turned out to be a bad idea to ask my coworkers to speak English.

When I requested that they switch to English so I could participate, they would make the discussion as brief as possible, than go on to cover the same issue among themselves at great length. At least, it seemed like that's what was happening. Not understanding Urdu or Malay, for all I know they could have been discussing baseball scores or swapping movie reviews, throwing in a technical term I was able to recognize once in a while so that the discussion would seem to be work-related. If this was the case, they were losing out. I've seen some really good movies and could definitely contribute.

A second reason requesting that English be spoken seems like a loser idea is that with a heightened sensitivity to issues involving race and language any attempt to deal with the matter might result in some kind of harassment or discrimination charge. If this happens there is always the threat of being required to attend sensitivity training or given a warning, which would be much worse than a little frustration over not being able to understand what coworkers were saying. There is also the possibility of generating resentment and friction in the group, a chance I didn't want to take.

The language disconnect has come to have a sort of "Emperor's New Clothes" aspect — many people know that it is a problem with potentially serious negative effects, but are afraid to point this out or try to deal with it due to possible backlash. No one wants to be the first one to point out that the emperor is naked.

A third reason to keep my thoughts carefully to myself is that in the last ten years an increasing number of managers I've worked for, as well as project leaders I've worked with, were not native English speakers. Raising the issue might seem insulting to them. It would be a serious misstep on my part to risk this reaction when a job review or request to participate in future projects could hang in the balance.

As it turns out, however, many people elsewhere are not as timid about confronting both sides of the issue. A December 12, 2012 article from the Associated Press notes that, according to the Equal Employment Opportunity Commission, complaints about discrimination based on speaking ability or foreign accents have increased by 76% between 1997 and 2011, totaling 11,800 complaints in 2011. Workers who allege discrimination against them based on their accent or national origin initiate many of these legal actions.

Employees who are union members may have some protection against retaliation for lodging complaints about language issues. However, in Silicon Valley not only do most tech jobs have no union protection, but California is an "at-will" employment state, meaning that as long as everyone is treated equally it is perfectly legal to fire workers at any time for any reason. Not making waves in order to get by is something of an art form here.

Balancing the conflicting interests of English speakers who need to understand what is being said around them and non-English speakers who communicate most fluently in their native language but have difficulty making themselves understood in English is a growing challenge for management, and one that does not seem to have a clear solution. Unfortunately, what it does seem to have is a high degree of tension on both sides of the fence.

Although my own frustration has led to some problems, at least these have only a limited scope as far as the harm they could do. If I don't understand why a change was made, if someone else spends hours ferreting out some information I could have provided, or problem determination work is duplicated needlessly, at least, as we often tell each other in moments of extreme pressure, no one is bleeding and no one is about to jump off a bridge.

However, there could be much more severe consequences in environments like hospitals and clinics, which now have as diverse a language base as high-tech among both the staff and patients. With instructions regarding patient care having to be communicated among caregivers with different language backgrounds, an error could mean that patient care is compromised. In an emergency situation, being able to communicate about exactly what is wrong very quickly could be a life-or-death matter.

Since the language disconnect is something that can't be changed, after experimenting with several ways of dealing with it I hit on a few tactics which seem to work out, at least to some degree. The first and most basic one is to constantly tell myself to calm down. Each time conversations in a language other than English start around me, my tension level seems to ratchet up. Am I missing something critical? Like a mantra, it helps to keep repeating the message to myself: calm down...calm down. On occasions when that doesn't seem to work, I close my eyes and think of the paychecks.

The second tactic is volunteering to either create or update any documentation required for changes I haven't been able to follow as the discussions involving them were under way. This works out well for all of us. The same issue of limited language skills that make my coworkers much better trouble-shooters and creative thinkers in their own language means they are usually happy to get some help with writing tasks. The benefit of this approach is that they are much more likely to keep me in the loop as problems are worked on so that written material can be ready to go when changes are finalized. This isn't an ideal solution, but is better than nothing.

The third way of dealing with language issues is, when in a position to select project participants, try to select coworkers who don't speak the same language. If a discussion is between someone who speaks Vietnamese and English but not Spanish, me, and someone who speaks Spanish and English but not Vietnamese, the discussions will be held in English, our only common language. This makes eavesdropping a much more fruitful activity, although it does have a potential down side if one or both of the other project participants do not communicate all that well in English.

Although these ways of coping help to get by, it is still isolating not to speak the language of the people around me, and there are a few situations I will probably never get used to.

When, during a one-on-one conversation with a coworker, a third person wanders over and starts discussing something in another language, I am suddenly turned into the dog again. What is being said? How to react? Wait it out? Go back to my own cube? Ask them to speak English? It is hard to believe that there is any country in the world where doing this isn't considered rude, but in my cubehood it is a common occurrence. Holding my temper and waiting it out, all I can say is: woof.

Like other annoyances, language issues can bother me a lot more when blood sugar is low, the stress level is already high, it's been a long day, or something critical is going wrong. In these situations, hearing a conversation launched that will leave me stranded in a fog may upset me enough to consider another of my go-to tactics: making up a reason to be away from my desk for a while, grabbing a notebook, and walking purposefully to another floor or building then back. It's a way to cool down, think carefully, and avoid saying something I'll regret. On quieter days with less going on, the language disconnect may barely bother me at all.

During these more relaxed times I can enjoy some of the interesting points about working with people from a multitude of different backgrounds. Hearing a guest worker from South Korea describing what citizens there really think about the "Dear Leader" in the north is an absolute hoot. Listening to tales of what it's like to live in a country with an institutionalized system of bribery for even the most minor transactions has provided a lot of insight into what life is like in India. Stories about long and difficult adventures from coworkers who were propelled into emigration from their home countries due to political oppression or natural disasters are eye-opening. Knowing what life is like elsewhere leaves me feeling grateful and lucky to be here.

It's been a long and interesting odyssey from the time many years ago when I first heard a foreign language spoken at work and stopped to listen to something so unfamiliar to the modern-day Tower of Babel. It was inconceivable then to think that someday the vast majority of people around me at work would be from other countries, turning me into a minority — and somewhat of a stranger in a familiar land.

Showboat

....

Disbelief. Utter disbelief. What Dana was describing would have been the perfect solution, but the deadline for the time when it could have been useful was long past.

Blocked several weeks ago by a problem which no one on the team trying to piece together a specialized package of hardware and software for a customer could figure out, we'd sent out email to anyone we thought could help. There were only a few people who had experience integrating components from the two vendors involved. Dana was one of them.

She hadn't answered any of the emails, but now, with a rapt audience and all eyes on her, was outlining how she had gotten past the problem where we had failed. Discreetly, I checked the emails that had been sent out requesting assistance. Yes, she was on the distribution list, and none of the emails that had been sent were returned as undeliverable. The details she was now going over might possibly have helped us get things working before the deadline for getting bids in had expired.

This meeting was the dreaded "post-action review," held when something has gone so wrong that merely slapping someone on the wrist isn't enough. Public flogging and humiliating admissions of incompetence were required. As the team lead my job right now was to be on the receiving end of the flogging-and-humiliating-admissions stage of the review, promising attendees from the sales department and other assorted managers to do everything humanly possible to avoid the same situation in the future.

The obvious question went unasked: why no response from Dana until today? Instead, the marketing manager was getting more irate by the minute. Dana had figured it out, what was wrong with us? Digging up the emails and pointing out that we'd asked for her help but gotten no reply would only make things worse, sounding like petulant excuses for our ineptness.

After eating the requisite amount of crow, collecting the usual number of management boot-marks on my rear, and offering abject apologies to the working-on-commission salespeople, whose Christmas was now going to be a little less merry because of my stupidity, I was allowed to leave. At least, I consoled myself, this isn't Japan — no one would expect me to fall on my sword for having failed. Tarnished as my reputation was, life would go on.

The post-action review was, unfortunately, always a possibility in pre-sales technical support, my current job. In this position, I was called on to provide a proof of concept backing up what the sales force, often in a delusional state caused by the prospect of serious money by way of commissions, had promised a customer would work.

Struggling to attempt to make good on these dollar-fueled technical fantasies often required rounding up people with specialized knowledge for help, as almost no one could single-handedly cover all aspects of large, complex configurations. Most of the time, people were helpful and understanding when asked for assistance. Occasionally, however, even with the company's financial health at stake there was some resistance.

Whatever had been behind Dana's unwillingness to share information when it could have been useful wasn't new. She'd not only declined to answer emails asking for help or opinions previously, but would do the same thing in conversations. No, no — she really didn't have any idea what was wrong, she'd have to think about it, she'd let us know.

Apparently those light bulbs over the heads of characters in comic strips representing ideas aren't just fiction, because once the spotlight was on her and the moment of maximum dramatic impact was at hand, the ideas would start to flow.

As annoying as this habit was, there was a great benefit for Dana in withholding information this way. When she finally did supply answers, whatever bits of wisdom she had to share seemed extremely valuable. If the same information had been shared easily and immediately when asked for, it would have appeared relatively unimportant.

Dana's way of handling things illustrated the difference between giving something away and demanding to be paid for it. Between coworkers, the sharing-when-asked model is a lot less painful for people on the receiving end of information, but makes a lot less of an impression. If it's true that "Knowledge is power," one of the manifestations of that power is forcing other people to jump through hoops to get access to that knowledge.

The occasional drama queen routine seemed a bit odd coming from Dana because she was otherwise very good to work with. As an individual contributor, her work was not only excellent but well-documented and easy to follow. Like almost all of the rest of the team, she was something of an introvert, keeping mostly to herself and seldom having lunch with coworkers or socializing. However, in a group of people whose idea of the perfect lunch hour is to sit alone quietly playing a video game or reading, she didn't stand out as being unusual.

In the past, I had seen a few situations where clinging to information other people needed made a lot of sense. At one company I'd worked for, as successive rounds of cutbacks took place management had implemented an interesting tactic guaranteed to insure not only withholding of information from coworkers, but extreme degrees of backstabbing and sabotaging.

They simply announced that every three months employees would be required to interview for their own jobs. Each department would be required to "hire" one less person during these quarterly reviews, effectively laying one person off. Pitting people in the same departments against each other in this way launched behavior similar to plots on "Survivor."

Even as we scrambled up résumés and started looking at jobs elsewhere, the sudden enmity between people who had worked together peacefully for years was heartbreaking. Reflecting what was going on with our company, the job market was bad right now. Being let go might mean a year or more of unemployment. With many of us in the mid-life years of children yet to get through college and parents who needed some financial help, people desperate to hang on were doing everything possible to undermine other department members. When that inevitable round of cuts was launched, someone like Dana was likely to be spared, whereas the person trying to get the bid put together who couldn't get the job done looked a lot more expendable.

However, the last-man-standing scenario that made "expertise hoarding" a perfectly logical tactic in that situation was not the setting within which Dana seemed to be acting out her occasional version of hide-and-seek with information.

As often happens in high-tech, the employment pendulum had swung over to the other side. It was a great job market, and not only was the company not laying off, but hiring experienced technicians had become difficult, with well-qualified candidates often getting several very good job offers. Managers would get nervous when someone took a few hours off and returned to work nicely dressed. Job security was good right now, but even so: Dana. How could we get her to be more cooperative?

When Dana's diva act appeared to be spinning up, the two levers that seemed to pry her participation loose without too much delay were intensely focused attention and a chance for visibility to upper management, which was a little strange because she appeared to have no interest in being promoted. With those considerations in mind, we eventually came up with a few ways to make working with her a little less painful.

Since recognition from people higher up the food chain was of concern to Dana, the first way of getting cooperation was to let her know that her contributions would be given star billing on any emails, documentation or other communications which would be widely distributed — if she could have the information available by the time these were sent out. Like other missives of those types it is unlikely that recipients even read them, but knowing that her name would be published and her contributions prominently credited almost always assured that those contributions would be provided without delay.

The second way of gaining cooperation was to give her a stage and audience to appear in front of. This worked out very well, as under these circumstances her performances were always relatively brief. The same information which, when provided by other team members would simply have been contained in documents was delivered in person by Dana, often with a dramatic flourish and accompanied by a brief PowerPoint or other visual aids. Shy as she could be most of the time, she did surprisingly well in front of an audience, and was a good public speaker.

In this situation, we scheduled her at the beginning of meetings and she often left after her performance. Like most good actresses, she had an intuitive understanding of when to exit the stage. Given the choice between getting her cooperation by providing her with a chance to bask in the limelight and another potential appearance at a post-action review, deciding what to do was an absolute no-brainer.

Speaking of no brainers: after the immediate pain wore off and I had a chance to think through the events that led up to the review, I came to agree with the management and sales departments. The failure had really been mine. Preoccupied with juggling so many pieces of a complicated project at one time, I had lost the big picture. My screw-up was not taking Dana's possible reluctance to share without the incentive of attention into account, even though her patterns were familiar. I hadn't approached her personally, asked for help, and offered the kind of public star turn that might have shaken loose the assistance which could have saved the project.

At least the public humiliation was behind me now. It was time to think ahead and start making plans for the next two projects waiting for technical configurations to be validated.

This time I would be better prepared. Not only would I be more careful about dealing with Dana and the few other people who required "special handling" methods, but I would also try to find a good recipe for crow — just in case.

Zoo, Too?

....

Enough about work. After all, even the worst day on the job ends eventually, and after however many hours of bubble-whacking and crazy-dodging the day entailed, you can pack it up and head out, leaving it all behind.

It would be nice to think that once the work day is over so is the need to exercise all that self-restraint and tact until tomorrow. Well, maybe — but maybe not. Since our personalities come everywhere with us, the darlings we can hardly wait to leave behind may well be lurking on the other end of that trip to various after-hours hangouts.

Different settings provide a wide range of opportunities for people to exercise their own brands of "special" behavior and self-expression. Since the people you're so happy to get away from aren't at work twenty-four hours a day either, they get plenty of chances to bring their personalities with them to other places.

Planning to escape the human tape players and passive-aggressives by heading over to the health club to get a little exercise? The "Gym Zoo" may have as many colorful characters as the office — talk about a pack of folks with some interesting quirks.

Ever watched the free-weight users working through their reps in front of a mirror? The admiration between some of them and their reflections is a sight to see, a look of deep adoration that would be prized by any lover. Hey, you and your reflection — get a room.

Then there are the exercisers who seem to be married to a particular piece of equipment, tying it up for ten or fifteen minutes, stepping away to let someone else work in, then immediately returning and embracing it with the enthusiasm of a long-lost friend. The "circuit trainers" who tie up five pieces of equipment and try to banish anyone else from access while they complete their circuits. The socializers, endlessly schmoozing while draped over a piece of equipment, oblivious to the hostile stares of people waiting to use it. The grunting weight-lifters, dramatically going through their groans and moans while hoisting barbells and ostentatiously dropping them. The appearance of the gym version of a Verbal Diarrhea Twin, happy to chat on and on while the limited time you have available for exercise ticks away. And let us not forget the ink-covered human canvasses blanketed by tattoos, who make anyone with tats over less than half of their bodies look a little effeminate by comparison. The impressive variety of gym rats definitely deserve their own book. My nomination for "Gym Zoo" authors are the one or two exercisers every gym seems to have, who show up every day at the same time and stay for hours.

Done with your workout and heading over to night school for a class or to your kids' junior high for open house? The ego-polishing, preening, and jockeying for position in the academic world can make the horn-bashing contest in "The Bachelor Herd" look like a genteel tea party by comparison. Maybe the rarefied air in those ivory towers causes some form of lightheadedness which spawns those heated debates on the meaning and competing interpretations of obscure passages in books which would be read exactly zero times if they weren't required for a class. Agree politely, nod, look interested, wait it out, move on. No reason to annoy someone who will be giving you — or your child — a grade.

Think you can avoid all of it by leaving work, the gym, and school behind and heading home? Nice try, but: homeowners associations. It seems to be an unwritten rule that in order to hold office in a homeowners' association, a petty authoritarian streak is required. Where do all these people come from whose mission in life is to knock on your door and inform you that your new beige curtains are just slightly outside of the range of beige acceptable in the development? That your grass is a micron too tall? That someone reported music coming from your house until 10:01 pm, when the official music curfew is 10:00 pm? As the age of automated monitoring has crept into the office, maybe homeowners associations are where Martina and her fellow enforcers have gone to satisfy their need to indulge in petty carping.

Although it can be tiring to deal with these personality issues in so many places, there can be some benefits. In the same way that learning to cope at work can help with other areas, coming up with ways to get past the assortment of head cases at the gym, school, or homeowners association may provide some interesting new insights.

Finding a graceful way to pry access to a machine away from the "circuit trainer" without causing animosity may help think of a way to deal with a software shithead jealously guarding his territory, or to get the tyrant guarding the office supply cabinet to part with a few notebooks or pens without having to secure permission from a fourth-level manager. Figuring out how to mollify the homeowners association representative knocking on your door and pointing out that your azaleas are planted too close to the curb may be an approach that can get the office watcher to quit carping about violations so petty that no one else would have even noticed the person who was using two inches more than the allotted cabinet space to store their cereal or box of tea bags.

At last, the reward for making it safely through your day. Finally, finally — home, that sanctuary where you can close the door behind you, shut out the world, and feel free to relax completely. Right? Well, that also depends. Married? Got kids? Got parents? For anyone with teenagers, critical in-laws, or continuously nagging spouses, the Office Zoo may be more than a way to make a living — it may actually be an escape from something more trying.

Luckily for me, my husband has no interest in writing his own book, since after attending family gatherings for years, listening to dozens of repetitions of cute childhood stories, tolerating criticism about his politics, and engaging in spirited debates on numerous topics with my siblings, he could easily write his own book — "The In-Law Zoo."

For all the joys of hearth and home, there are good reasons why "alone on a deserted island" is still such a popular and enduring escapist fantasy.

Epilog

·················

Even though the daily trip through the gauntlet of situations at work can be an exercise in survival, it can also occasionally be something much better. Work may provide structure, the confidence that comes with mastering new things, participation in creative projects, the deep satisfaction of being on a team that works well and possibly some enjoyment of the people around us. Even given the caution needed when considering that a coworker might be promoted to a position of authority, many close friendships began between people who were coworkers. Good and bad, the types of different experiences at work are as unlimited as the types of people we have to get along with.

This book is a glance at some of those people, but there are too many variations of the human animal to consider them all. However, for both the zoo members described and the ones left out the same general methods of coping hold true. There are always benefits to stepping back, taking a deep breath, thinking carefully about a situation, and making a clear-headed, logical and well-thought-out decision about how to proceed before realizing it's hopeless, throwing in the towel, and running frantically for the exit.

Or, as more commonly happens, realizing it's hopeless, thinking about throwing in the towel and heading for the exit, but then remembering how necessary those paychecks are and deciding to stick it out. Tethered to our jobs by financial gravity, there is only so far that mental images of the bolt for freedom will let us go before being yanked up short by thoughts of grocery bills and mortgage payments. At least until the house is paid off, the kids are out of school, and the retirement savings balance gives you the financial green light, the angel on one shoulder recommending the calm return to your cube will, hopefully, win out over the devil on your other shoulder urging you to ignore your internal censor, tell that clown who just asked you to do something phenomenally stupid just where to stick it, and storming out. And for those occasions when the angel seems to be losing the argument, try this: imagine how well the sudden change in job status to "unemployed" will go over with your family.

For those of us repeatedly going through the bolt-for-the-door scenario, suggestions like the ones in this book on survival at the lower rungs of the food chain may have more practical value than advice offered by empower-and-conquer self-help book industry titans. The problem with those books is that, by definition, the ones that get published are written by people for whom things worked out. Does anyone think there would be much of a market for books like "How I Risked It All, Lost It All, And Wound Up Living Under A Bridge," or "How To Try Something Spectacular And Wind Up A Humiliated Failure"?

The authors of books that do get printed, the "Gee Look At Successful Me" authors, invariably describe how to make a pile of money and ascend to spectacular heights by doing things like thinking outside the box, coming up with the next hot cloud application, or quitting a day job to start a world-changing mega-whatever.

However, for every book author who made it, there are probably thousands of attempted-success stories for whom "out of the box" also means "outside of any discernible possibility of success." These unfortunates may see their ideas crash and burn when actually tested, may get their ideas stolen by some shark or hacker, or wind up watching in frustration as the highly publicized launch of the next big mega-whatever goes the way of Pets.com, the spectacularly failed web site that was going to revolutionize the way people buy pet supplies. These failures may leave people spending the next umpteen years paying off bills they ran up and loans they took out, and send venture capitalists back to investors with explanations and apologies.

The "Success Industry" authors often throw in a few words about persevering through adversity on the way to making enough money to afford a fleet of cars, but if things hadn't turned out well in the end, they'd be working shifts at Wal-Mart instead of presuming to tell the rest of us that, hey, it's easy, anyone can do it — just buy my book for a set of sure-fire instructions on how to succeed. Right. If that approach really worked we could all get rich and famous by, as one book advocated, mindlessly aping the habits of successful people.

If there is one bit of advice that seems worth following consistently for career bottom-dwellers, it would be this: suck up to everyone, because you never know. Things are very fluid in high-tech, and that furious tirade you unleashed on the clumsy post-college puppy who screwed up the back-end storage arrays may come back to haunt you some day. In a few years, he could wind up being a hiring manager looking over your application. When that day comes, he'll remember how you reacted.

Carefully watching how things work out in the real world for real people can be very instructive, as can thinking long and hard about what is really to be gained, lost, or risked when trying to move up the ladder, strike out on your own, or test the waters with that interesting startup.

When pondering these steps, it's worth a good long hard stare in the psychological mirror. Sometimes it can be hard to tell the difference between what you really want and what you have been convinced to think you want by peer pressure, popular culture, family traditions, or expectations pumped up and manipulated by advertising.

At heart, many people just aren't that ambitious, regarding work as part of the framework of their lives but not the most important part. The self-help guides advocating upward mobility for everyone seem to look down on people who regard work mainly as a way to make a living in order to enjoy their families in peace and quiet, and offer snidely dismissive opinions about anyone who opts to quit work and stay home with their children. I've known many under-the-radar oar-pullers who turn in excellent work year after year, are great to be around, seem content to stay put, and are not looking to move up the chain to more complicated and demanding jobs even when offers are extended.

The flip side of all those miserable coworkers who bring personal issues to work with them and find endless ways to express their unhappiness are the quiet, steady, consistent colleagues who are happy with what's waiting for them outside of work and seldom cause drama. Maybe in addition to interviewing job applicants about their technical skills, we should ask to talk to their families. Although this would probably be illegal, it might provide a lot of useful information.

Speaking of useful information, what about me? Although it would seem like the self-awareness gained by living through the experiences in this book would have raised my consciousness about my own behavior enough to avoid doing anything that would annoy my coworkers or my husband, well, let's just politely say that I'm working on it.

My energy goes into trying to keep my head down, get through the day in one piece, and coexist peacefully with everyone. As far as I know, it's been a while since anyone else's serious work meltdown has been traceable to me, and things are generally calm in my cubehood at a large tech company.

Since I'm not yet quite perfect, it's fortunate that my husband, that former bachelor herd member, is willing to listen patiently to the same stories several times, wait it out while I'm venting about things it would be either politically incorrect or unwise to share with coworkers, and be counted on to agree wholeheartedly about how unreasonable people he's never met are.

Without knowing what the other side of an issue is, he is always on my side, carefully sympathizing and waiting for me to wind down, listening attentively while I tell him about the day's journey through the Office Zoo.

About the Author & Artist

LEE WELLINGTON is a pen name for the author who, after 35 years of employment at companies including Hewlett Packard, IBM, and Intel, is still reporting to work every day in the storage division of a large corporation. She has never held a job which her parents understand.

MARY PAQUET, however, is real. She lives in San Jose, California, and is a mixed media artist specializing in figurative, landscape, cityscape, and still life. Her paintings have been displayed in numerous galleries. Mary is Past President of the Santa Clara Valley Watercolor Society. Her art can be viewed at: http://mary-artadventures.blogspot.com/

The Office Zoo is available as an ebook on Kindle; in print at Amazon.com; and at my Createspace eStore https://www.createspace.com/4516724 (where I make the most royalties).